MULTIPLYING OUR HUMAN POTENTIAL

THE END OF IGNORANCE

JOHN MIGHTON

ALFRED A. KNOPF CANADA

PUBLISHED BY ALFRED A. KNOPF CANADA

Copyright © 2007 John Mighton

All rights reserved under International and Pan-American Copyright Conventions. No part of this book may be reproduced in any form or by any electronic or mechanical means, including information storage and retrieval systems, without permission in writing from the publisher, except by a reviewer, who may quote brief passages in a review. Published in 2007 by Alfred A. Knopf Canada, a division of Random House of Canada Limited. Distributed by Random House of Canada Limited, Toronto.

Knopf Canada and colophon are trademarks.

www.randomhouse.ca

Pages 311 to 312 constitute a continuation of the copyright page.

Library and Archives Canada Cataloguing in Publication

Mighton, John, 1957–
The end of ignorance : multiplying our human potential / John Mighton.

ISBN 978-0-676-97962-6

1. Learning ability. 2. Intellect. 3. Mathematical ability.
4. Education—Aims and objectives. 5. Education—Philosophy.
6. Interdisciplinary approach in education. I. Title.

LB14.7.M53 2007   370.1   C2007-900349-4

Text design: CS Richardson

First Edition

Printed and bound in the United States of America

2 4 6 8 9 7 5 3 1

CONTENTS

—

CHAPTER ONE

THE WASTE ETHIC

—

TWENTY-FIVE YEARS AGO, when I was studying philosophy at McMaster University, I wanted to write a book called "The Waste Ethic," which I hoped would be the first attempt in the history of the social sciences to accurately measure the amount of time people waste at work. I wasn't interested in simply tracking the time wasted by people who hate their jobs or who are totally unqualified for their positions. I wanted to find out what proportion of our work goes into producing, marketing and disposing of the vast array of products that, before the advent of mass media, nobody knew they needed or wanted. I never did find time to write that book, but having spent the past twenty years teaching mathematics to thousands of children and teenagers—both gifted and challenged, and from both affluent and impoverished homes—I think I have a better idea of why we as a society are so efficient at wasting time.

It seems to me that two kinds of ignorance are always at work in our society, one extremely destructive and the other healthy. My career in theatre was initially shaped by the first kind of ignorance, in ways I am only beginning to understand. I came to writing plays rather late in life because I grew up thinking that to be an artist you needed to be born with a special gift. It wasn't until I read Sylvia Plath's letters to her mother and saw how as a teenager she had learned her craft in small, determined steps, dismantling poems like motors to see how they worked and writing imitations of the things she loved, that I began to believe there was a path I could follow to develop a voice of my own.

The destructive form of ignorance has divided many societies: it is the ignorance that says there are fundamental, inborn differences between people, between peasants and nobility or minorities and majorities. It is this ignorance that leads us, even in this affluent age, to neglect the majority of children by educating them in schools in which only a small minority are expected to naturally love or excel at learning.

Two years ago, during a visit to the York Detention Centre, I saw the effects of this ignorance in its most devastating form. I had been asked to teach a lesson in mathematics to a group of teenagers who were awaiting trial and who were not thrilled to be spending their afternoon doing math. I told the students I had once struggled with mathematics myself and I promised to try to make the subject more interesting and easier than they might remember from school. I reassured them that if they didn't understand something in my lesson it would be my fault for not explaining it properly, so they could ask me to explain it again. The teenagers responded to my promise exactly as I have seen young children respond: they raced through their worksheets and called for the tutors to give them extra work. One girl, whom I had heard complaining at the beginning of the lesson, made me put a check mark beside each of her answers. When I finished she said, "I've never had that in my life. I've only had this," and she wrote a large X across her page.

The letter X is a fitting symbol for our failure to care for those individuals who, like the girl at the detention centre, happen to struggle or fall behind in school or in life. The crossed lines evoke the barriers we place, out of ignorance and indifference, between the majority of children and their unrealized potential. But the letter X is also a universal sign for a different and potentially redeeming kind of ignorance: in the sciences and in mathematics, it is the letter most commonly used to stand for the unknown.

Einstein once wrote:

> The most beautiful and deepest experience one can have is the sense of the mysterious . . . One who has never had this experience seems to me if not dead, then at least blind. To sense that behind anything that can be experienced there is something that our mind cannot grasp and whose beauty and sublimity reaches us only indirectly and as a feeble reflection, this is religiousness. In this sense I am religious.

The sense of the mysterious that Einstein described can define a person as much as their sense of courage or integrity or charity. People who experience the ineffable mystery of the world also tend to have a deep sense of humility, as Socrates demonstrated when he admitted how little he knew to the Athenians who put him on trial for his life. This sense of the mysterious drives such people to pull aside the veil or wipe away the fog that separates them from the mystery.

Every child who is well cared for naturally develops a sense of the mysterious. The feeling that behind every door another world is waiting can make a child's world a paradise. But, once at school, children often begin to lose their sense of the hidden beauty of the world. By having to compete and be compared to their peers, many lose faith in their intelligence and their imagination; by having to struggle so hard to keep up, many come to believe that the world is beyond their understanding. The magical world that they once inhabited begins to recede until they can see no point in dreaming about or searching for anything beyond the world of their immediate needs and desires.

People are often surprised when I tell them that I am a mathematician as well as a playwright. Some people seem to believe that the brain can hold only one kind of information, or that when one side is working the other has to be left empty for storage. If they are lucky, students graduating from high school will likely believe that they have only one or two talents and that the majority of subjects offered at school are either uninteresting or beyond their grasp. As a society we are living under a vast spell or illusion. We have effectively hypnotized ourselves, but not in a single performance. It has taken twelve or thirteen years of school to put us in a suggestive state so that we all believe more in our limitations than in our potential, and it is difficult for anyone to snap their fingers to break the trance.

When I was a teenager I read a fair number of biographies of scientists and mathematicians. These biographies always gave me the impression that a person had to be born with a gift for mathematics and that someone who had this gift would never do badly on a test or struggle to learn a concept. This belief sank in very deeply; like many young people I would often give up on things because I was afraid of coming up against my limitations. It wasn't until I was in my thirties that I had the courage to go back to school and study mathematics.

At university I had an enormous advantage over the other first-year students: I had been tutoring math for several years to supplement my income as a playwright, and I knew the high school material inside out. I had also learned some of the university material in advance. But occasionally I would do badly on a test and I would be paralyzed by insecurity. I remember lying in bed after I had failed one test, thinking that I had reached a threshold I couldn't go beyond and that I would have to give up my ambitions. My work as a tutor had given me a great deal of perspective on the issue of ability, but I still couldn't get over those fears. It took several years before I began to notice that the things I had found impossible on a particular test became trivial once I had a chance to practise and learn them properly. I began to wonder how many people have stopped themselves out of fear of failure from developing talents in things they found interesting when they were young.

Nine years ago I was looking for a way to give something back to my local community. It occurred to me that I should try to help kids who needed help with math. Mathematicians don't always make the best teachers because mathematics has become obvious to them; they can have trouble seeing why their students are having trouble. But because I had struggled with math myself, I wasn't inclined to blame my students if they couldn't move forward. If a student didn't understand my explanation I assumed there was something wrong with the explanation, not with the student.

Many of my closest friends are actors. Actors often have a good deal of time on their hands and they will do anything for attention, so I was able to convince a group of my friends, even the ones who had dropped out of math, that they too could tutor math. We started an after-school tutoring program in my apartment called JUMP (Junior Undiscovered Math Prodigies).

The JUMP program was founded on a very lucky accident. I had asked the principal of a local school to send some kids to the program who were having trouble with math. She misunderstood me and delivered the most challenged kids in the school, including a number of kids in special education classes who were performing far below grade level.

Working with these children, and with the thousands of children I have taught since JUMP started, has been one of the most inspiring things I have done. I am now convinced that the brain can develop new abilities more readily than traditional theories of intelligence allow, and that children who face challenges at school are capable of far more than we expect of them. Many of the students from the first few years of JUMP had moved into academic classes by the time they entered high school. And thanks to the work of hundreds of teachers and volunteers, JUMP is now an in-class program that delivers the complete curriculum in mathematics from Grades 1 to 8. JUMP materials and methods are being used with encouraging results in several hundred schools in Canada, the United States, Australia, South Africa and Britain (which is home to the world's largest single JUMP program, with five thousand children).

In this book I will describe the methods and results of the JUMP program, but this is not primarily a book about JUMP, or even about mathematics. The examples I give illustrate broader points about the way we educate children and about the expectations we have of weaker students. It is possible to apply the methods I describe to various subjects. Deep psychological principles, which are as important as the curriculum or the content of the course, must be taken into account in the teaching of any subject: including the way children perceive themselves in groups and the way cognitive abilities can be developed by playing with subtle variations on patterns. I argue that, because we have ignored these principles, our educational system is far from optimal and the means we have developed to educate children are extremely inefficient.

The philosopher Wittgenstein said that people get themselves into trouble when they fail to pay attention to the precise meanings of words. I argue that many inefficiencies in education stem from confusions over the meaning of some words used in educational theory. These confusions are not of academic or philosophical interest alone: they have had a profound effect in our schools.

It is not easy to describe the things I have seen in the educational system, or the ideas behind JUMP, without oversimplifying. I often return to the same idea several times to provide a different angle or perspective. It is almost impossible to say anything in education that is not both true and false at the same time. The things that children respond to are often surprising and counterintuitive, and words and categories can fail to capture the complexity of a child's behaviour. It is easy to attach a label to a particular style or philosophy of teaching, but I hope that educators will wait until they have read the whole book before they try to classify or name the methods I describe in this book. One of the greatest threats to education is educational theory that does not take account of the extraordinary complexity of the mind or of the subtleties in what children find interesting and meaningful and in what motivates them to learn.

When I was growing up I often dreamed about becoming a good mathematician or a good writer, but never about becoming a good teacher. Given a choice, I prefer sitting alone in my office doing mathematics to teaching, giving talks about mathematics or writing workbooks for children. But over the past ten years I have effectively given up my careers in math and the theatre to work forty to fifty hours a week as a volunteer for JUMP. And there are several reasons why I have set aside my other work in order to teach and develop educational materials.

I think it is fair to say that there has been no great improvement in the state of education in the past thirty years. And over the same period, despite the substantial efforts of governments and charities, there has been no significant improvement in the condition of the world's poor. At the same time, a succession of breakthroughs in productivity and in technology has transformed our society and created vast fortunes around the world. When so much has changed in contemporary society, how have the state of education and the level of poverty remained the same? I believe our lack of progress in these two areas is connected.

Poverty has never been eliminated, even in the wealthiest societies, because its source has remained invisible even to the enlightened or progressive eye. In trying to eradicate poverty we have never taken into account the destructive effects of the most basic tenet of education—shared by socialist and conservative societies alike—that children are born with vastly different mental abilities and that the majority can never be expected to reason or think clearly about mathematics and the natural world. I will argue that intellectual poverty, which societies have imposed on the majority of children out of ignorance of their real potential, is the deepest source of material poverty, because it makes societies incapable of distributing their wealth in a fair, rational or sustainable manner.

If we are ever to nurture the full potential of children, we must develop a model of education based on a deeper understanding of the brain. In the natural sciences our understanding of complex systems such as the brain has recently undergone a paradigm shift. Scientists now recognize that complex systems show emergent behaviour: new and unexpected properties of a system can emerge out of nowhere from a series of small changes. For example, if a chemist adds a reagent to a chemical solution one drop at a time, nothing may appear to be happening until, with the addition of just one more drop, the whole solution spontaneously changes colour. I have seen this behaviour in hundreds of students: they can appear to be at the limits of their ability, and then, with a single drop of knowledge, they leap to a new level of understanding.

Based on my observations of thousands of students, I am now convinced that new intellectual abilities can emerge in any student from a series of small advances, and that mathematics, rather than being the most difficult subject, is one in which a teacher can most easily add, rigorously and effectively, the drops of knowledge that can transform a student. New discoveries in cognition and genetics suggest that the brain is much more plastic than scientists had previously imagined, and that with rigorous training, new neural connections and mental capacities can be developed even in older children and adults.

When I wrote *The Myth of Ability*, I hoped that some of its ideas would be tested in the school system. This has recently started to happen, particularly in school boards in western

Canada and in Britain. I have now had an opportunity to observe how the school system works at many levels, from classrooms to the offices of senior bureaucrats and ministers. While I have been inspired by the work of many outstanding teachers, administrators and educational theorists and consultants, I have also observed serious organizational flaws and conflicts of interest in some school boards and education ministries that prevent teachers and administrators from adopting and testing new programs in a scientific spirit. I believe these problems can be fixed, but this may take advocacy by the teachers who have been forced by their boards to work with ineffective textbooks and programs, and by the parents whose children have suffered as a result.

Teachers work under difficult conditions, with oversized classes and a growing number of responsibilities outside the classroom. None of the suggestions in this book are intended as criticisms of teachers, who in my opinion are engaged in heroic work. I developed the JUMP program because I saw so many teachers struggling to teach in large, diverse classrooms, with training and materials that were not designed to take into account the difficult conditions in those classrooms. My hope is that some of the ideas in this book may help make the jobs of teachers easier and more enjoyable.

I present a number of proposals for improving our schools and for introducing teaching methods that will allow teachers to nurture the non-linear potential in their students. I look closely at the philosophical and institutional barriers that prevent innovation in school systems, and also present success stories from schools in Canada and Britain that have introduced methods of teaching based on the assumption that abilities can be nurtured in all students.

Given the overwhelming scale of the problems we face in education and the persistently high levels of ignorance and poverty in the world, it is easy to become convinced that there is nothing an individual can do to make a difference. But, thankfully, the world itself is complex and prone to emergent behaviour. If we are willing to take the first step, to add the first drop, the ripples may spread more widely than we could ever have imagined.

—

CHAPTER TWO

THE EMERGENT MIND

—

In the spring of 2004, a year after the publication of *The Myth of Ability*, I received a letter from a doctor asking if I would talk to the mother of one of his patients. I don't usually consult with parents whose children aren't in the JUMP program, unless they happen to be friends or relatives whom I can't avoid, but the mother sounded as if she was at her wit's end. Her nine-year-old son, Matthew, had been assessed as being in the 0.1 percentile in mathematical ability (this means, on average, that he would test lower than 999 out of one thousand kids), and he was having a very rough time at school. Matthew's doctor wasn't sure he would ever develop a sense of numbers: even at age nine, after a great deal of specialized help and therapy, he seemed to have little sense of the relative size or order of numbers, and he could only add pairs of small numbers consistently. I found out later that Matthew, who is autistic, was so anxious about math that he would regularly throw up at school; in the six months before I received his doctor's letter, he had not been able to attend a single lesson in the subject.

Had I known that Matthew's fear of mathematics could make him physically ill, I'm not sure how things would have gone in our first tutorial. When he arrived with his mother at my apartment, I was nervous enough as it was. I wasn't certain that the fairly simple methods I had developed to help students in special education classes would work with a child who faced so many challenges. Had I been aware of the full extent of Matthew's anxiety, I'm not sure I would have agreed to see him.

For Matthew's first lesson I had decided to use an approach that works well with children who have lost their confidence in math. When children fall behind at school or when they are placed in special education classes, they often lose interest in the work they are assigned, because they know it is for less able students. Matthew had only ever been given simple exercises with concrete materials and basic number drills at school, but nothing had stuck. At nine he still couldn't do the simplest calculations with coins or blocks or even his fingers.

I told Matthew that I assumed he was very intelligent, so I would skip him ahead a few grade levels. I said that even though he was in Grade 4, I would teach him how to add fractions, which is something children don't usually learn to do until Grade 6 or 7. I've found that young children can get very excited about adding fractions: many have heard that fractions are difficult and that much older people, including their parents, have trouble understanding them. Indeed, many adults remember their introduction to numerators and denominators as the event that ended their career in mathematics.

I started by showing Matthew how to name fractions by counting the number of shaded pieces in a pie diagram. To find the numerator of a fraction (the top number, in case you've forgotten) you count the number of shaded pieces; to find the denominator you count the number of pieces in the whole pie. After he had practised this skill, with pictures I showed Matthew why, when you add a pair of fractions, you add the numerators but the denominator stays the same. After he had successfully added several pairs of fractions, such as 1/4 + 1/4, Matthew was clearly growing more confident—and so was I, so I decided I would take a risk. I asked him if he could add a triple sum: 1/7 + 1/7 + 1/7.

Over the past thirty years I have worked with hundreds of children who have struggled with math, including many children with attention deficits and behavioural problems. I have had a great deal of success in changing behaviour and building confidence by using a simple technique that, for lack of a better term, I call "raising the bar." When students have mastered a skill or concept, I simply raise the bar slightly by challenging them to answer a question that is only incrementally more difficult or complex than the one previously assigned. Children become very excited when they succeed in meeting a series of graduated challenges, and this excitement allows them to focus and take risks in their work.

At age nine, most children can figure out how to add three or more fractions by extending the method they learned to add a pair, even if they can't explicitly state the rule: "You add the top numbers and the bottom stays the same." But when Matthew saw the triple sum he panicked, suddenly talking to himself in a stream of sentences that were too rapid and disconnected for me to follow. I began to panic myself, thinking I had lost him for the lesson, and I quickly took away the sheet of paper on which I'd written the fractions. After I had apologized and told him it was my fault for confusing him, he appeared to relax a little. But he continued to talk to himself, and I had no idea how I could regain his confidence. It was clear that I couldn't ask him to add fractions with larger numerators, as he could add only extremely small numbers such as $1 + 1$ and $1 + 2$. It occurred to me that the only way I could raise the bar for Matthew would be to increase the size of the denominators. I said, "Matthew, you're very smart. Could you add these fractions?" and I wrote

$$\frac{1}{17} + \frac{1}{17}$$

When he had written the answer—2/17—I said, "You're amazing! Could you add these?"

$$\frac{1}{39} + \frac{1}{39}$$

When he had answered that question, I said, "You're in big trouble now. I'll have to give you these."

$$\frac{1}{73} + \frac{1}{73}$$

As I continued to increase the size of the denominators, Matthew became more and more excited. After he had successfully added a pair of fractions with denominators in the hundreds, he was beside himself. Clearly overjoyed to be able to do a calculation involving such enormous numbers, he said, "I think I can do that other question." So I wrote

$$\frac{1}{7} + \frac{1}{7} + \frac{1}{7}$$

—and he quickly gave me the answer: 3/7.

This may seem like a very small victory, but for Matthew it was something of a new experience. He had solved the problem subconsciously. For the first time, perhaps in years, his intellect wasn't paralyzed by his fear of mathematics and he was able to draw on the processing power of his unconscious mind.

Several months after Matthew took this first step forward, I was asked to speak to a group of doctors who specialized in early childhood development at the Hospital for Sick Children in Toronto. Matthew's doctor and his mother had noticed some striking changes in him, particularly in his ability to focus and his willingness to attempt tasks that he had previously found impossible. He also seemed to be learning at a quicker rate many things he had previously struggled with.

Matthew now attends math classes at school. After approximately seventy tutorials (fewer lessons than you would get in a year of school), he has advanced four or five grade levels in many areas of the curriculum. He has begun to develop a sense of numbers that has transferred into his daily life. Six months ago he corrected his mother on how much time was left before he had to leave the house and he can now calculate and make change with money. His skills with fractions and with operations such as multiplication and division are better than in many older students I have worked with. In a recent lesson he was able to tell me which two-digit numbers are prime and which are composite, and he was able to draw factor trees for a variety of numbers.

Had I been able to teach Matthew five times a week for a full hour during the school day, rather than once a week for forty minutes in the evening, I believe he would have progressed much more quickly. And had I been a more able teacher, he would undoubtedly have gone even further. Matthew is one of the most challenging students I have met, as his brain appears to be extremely compartmentalized: he can learn a concept in one form and then have trouble applying that concept when it appears in a slightly different context or representation. Recently I have begun to develop some new approaches, which I will describe later in this book, that appear to be helping Matthew to develop conceptual abilities. But in spite of many encouraging breakthroughs in our lessons, I still feel that I am only beginning to understand how to teach him.

Matthew is not the first student I have taught who had severe difficulties in math, although the level of his anxiety was unique. Since JUMP started, in 1998, I have worked with more than a hundred children in special education classes and hundreds of other children who were struggling in regular classes. My work with these children has been particularly inspiring to me. It has exposed me to things I wouldn't have believed if I hadn't seen them, and has caused me to change my views of intelligence. I have likely learned more from these students than they will ever learn from me.

When I first started tutoring twenty years ago, I taught a boy who was in a Grade 6 special education class. That student has recently finished a doctorate in mathematics and has made some extremely interesting discoveries in the field, so I have become quite jealous of him. When I began teaching him, I couldn't see why he had been placed in a special education class, as he didn't appear to have any real challenges. His problems at school seemed to stem more from boredom and lack of confidence. And this was true of most of the students I taught before I started JUMP.

Nothing in my work as a professional tutor prepared me for the students who arrived in my apartment on the first day of JUMP. In *The Myth of Ability* I told the story of Lisa and several other students whom I taught in the first three years of the program. For my first lesson I had decided to teach fractions, and Lisa was the first student to arrive. Even though she was in Grade 6, I quickly found that she couldn't even count to ten by twos, and she had never heard of multiplication. She had been placed in a class for children who were mildly intellectually delayed, and every time I said something she would look at me like a deer in the headlights and say, "I don't understand what you are saying." I remember that lesson clearly as one of the turning points in my life. It was Lisa's paralyzing fear of mathematics, which I have since found to be widespread among children who struggle at school, and her inability to do the simplest calculations that forced me, from sheer necessity, to develop the techniques that have become the foundation of the JUMP program.

Three years after our first lesson, Lisa transferred from the remedial stream into an academic Grade 9 math program. In the second semester of that school year she skipped ahead and finished Grade 10 academic math. After attending JUMP tutorials only once or twice a week for four years, she had moved from testing at a Grade 1 level in math to an academic level a year ahead of her other studies.

In the same year that Lisa moved into the academic stream, the JUMP program moved out of my apartment and into several Toronto schools. But I continued to tutor several of the students who had started in the first year. Of the five students I kept in touch with or tutored after the program moved out of my apartment, four moved from special education classes into academic math classes (I believe the fifth could have moved to a higher level, but the school discouraged her mother from placing her daughter in the academic stream). One boy, who was in a Grade 5 special education class when he started JUMP, progressed so quickly that by Grade 7 he received a mark of 91 percent in a regular class—and his teacher told his mother he was the smartest kid in the

class. Another girl, who began with JUMP in Grade 6, finished calculus and has been a JUMP tutor herself for the past
two years. This year she was accepted to math programs at a
number of universities, including the University of Toronto.

In the fall of 2003 I had an opportunity to try out some of
the methods I had developed in the one-on-one program in
a regular class. Several teachers at a public school in Toronto
who had seen their students' progress in our after-school
program invited us to place some tutors in the classroom
and asked us to provide them with training and materials
that would help them teach math. Until then I had thought
JUMP would have to be only an after-school program. Since
the children in the program often had severe attention
deficits and learning disabilities, I thought they needed one-
on-one attention in order to learn anything. But within a few
weeks of working in a classroom, I knew it would be possible, and even easier in many ways, to help weaker students
in that setting.

That fall a Grade 3 teacher invited me to teach the math
lesson to her class for five weeks to test some of the methods
I had developed. I taught her students the material that
eventually became the JUMP fractions unit (which can be
downloaded from the JUMP website for free). There are two
versions of the fractions unit, one that we recommend for
Grades 3 and 4 and one for higher-level classes. Even though
I was teaching a Grade 3 class, I used the higher-level unit
because I wanted to see how far the class could go with the
material. Several of the children had been diagnosed as slow
learners and several had attention deficits; very few knew

how to multiply or even to add and subtract with real proficiency. Naturally I was nervous at first that I had been too ambitious in my choice of materials.

At the end of the five weeks all the children, including the ones who had attention deficits, sat in absolute silence for thirty minutes as they wrote their final exam. On the exam they had to name fractions, add and subtract fractions, reduce fractions, change mixed fractions to improper fractions (and vice versa), add mixed fractions, compare fractions for size and solve simple word problems involving fractions. Because at least half the class hadn't known any times tables when I started the lessons, the denominators in most of the questions were divisible by two, three, four or five (the children had learned how to multiply and divide by these numbers over the month). Otherwise the test covered operations with fractions that are normally taught in Grade 7 in Ontario. All the students scored more than 90 percent on the exam, and more than half scored 100 percent. The students who missed the test nagged me until I let them write it: for them the test was a chance to show what they had learned.

In the 2005–06 school year, twenty teachers in Winnipeg took part in a JUMP pilot organized by teachers, school board administrators and staff in the provincial ministry of education. Wendy Barkman, who was president of the Manitoba Association of Resource Teachers (MART) at the time, sent us the following comments from teachers who took part in the pilot:

Even my weakest students—who are functioning at a Grade 1 level in a Grade 5 classroom—are successful and keeping up with the rest of the class. Comments such as "I am smart," "Math is easy," and "I am great" are being voiced.

For the first time in my teaching career I have challenged students who are being successful at math and are keen and eager to do math. They are approaching the math class with the same eager anticipation as any high audience.

Finally a resource that excites not only teachers but students. To see the face of not one, not two, but twenty-seven students succeeding and enjoying math is so gratifying. Any student can have success! Class involvement increased.

In 2004 twelve teachers in inner-city schools in Toronto took part in a month-long pilot that was observed by students from the Ontario Institute for Studies in Education at the University of Toronto (OISE/UT). After the pilot the teachers were asked to rate, on a scale of 1 to 5, how much they thought they had underestimated the weakest students in their class, where 5 meant "greatly underestimated." Ratings were given in ten categories that included enthusiasm for math, ability to remember number facts, ability to concentrate, willingness to ask for harder work and ability to keep up with faster students. In every category, all of the teachers circled 4 or 5. A second pilot, observed by education students from Brock University, gave similar results with a different set of questions about weaker students' abilities.

Over the past five years, I have taught in regular public schools as well as in inner-city schools, private schools and First Nations schools. My observations, along with the reports I have received from hundreds of teachers and tutors who used the JUMP fractions unit or our workbooks for the standard curriculum, have led me to believe that we must change our expectations of weaker students. The extreme differences between the weakest and strongest students in our schools are, in my opinion, a product of the way the children are taught. All kids will never be the same, but I now believe that virtually all of them can do math at a level well beyond what we currently expect. While I teach mainly math, I have taught many other subjects as well, including English, physics, chemistry, economics, formal logic, philosophy and creative writing. And I believe that the striking improvements I have seen students make in math can occur in any other subject as well.

The idea that all kids can do well in math, or in any subject, is foreign to our culture. People are inclined to talk about innate gifts in any field, but their opinions about intelligence are most evident when they talk about mathematics. Math is widely thought to be a subject for which either you are born with ability or you aren't. People who can't read usually try to hide this fact, but people who can't do math are happy to reveal publicly how innumerate they are, particularly in stores and restaurants. Many are even proud of not knowing how to calculate simple percentages or add up a bill. No real stigma is attached to being bad at math: to be embarrassed about your inability to do math would be like being embarrassed about the colour of your eyes—it's something you're born with.

When I give talks on education I often ask the audience to raise their hands if they think they were born to be mathematicians or believe they could have worked in the subject had they wanted to. Even when I am speaking to groups of teachers, 10 percent at most put up their hands. Many people are convinced that there is a gene for mathematics. This gene seems to come with an expiry date, though, and most people can remember the year it gave out—when they had a particularly bad experience with the subject.

People cling stubbornly to the idea that children will excel in a subject only if they are blessed with the right genes, in spite of all the evidence from early childhood development that contradicts the notion of inborn abilities. Our views of what kids can and can't do are generally based on very old science. However, in a recent series of experiments that will likely revolutionize our understanding of heredity, scientists have begun to clarify the role played by an important biological system—the epigenome—in controlling human development.

The epigenome is an array of chemical markers and switches attached to the DNA molecule that helps switch on and off the expression of particular genes in the DNA. Recent experiments have shown that the molecules in the epigenome, which effectively control an animal's genetic destiny, can be altered significantly by its diet, its environment and even the way it is nurtured. Changes in the epigenome can cause changes in the DNA molecule itself, and these changes are inheritable, capable of being passed down over many generations. As the pharmacologist Moshe Szyf said recently,

> People used to think that once your epigenetic code was laid down in early development, that was it for life. But life is changing all the time and the epigenetic code that controls your DNA is turning out to be the mechanism through which we change along with it. Epignetics tell us that the little things in life can have an effect of great magnitude.

These new findings may help explain the growing body of research in early childhood development that shows that the brains of infants are sculpted more by their environment than by their DNA. According to the study "How are the Children?," "the impact of experience on cognitive ability is significantly more powerful than the influence of heredity." Neurologists have found that even the brains of genetic twins can become wired very differently if the twins are raised in different environments. In many countries this new appreciation of the plasticity of the infant brain has led to calls for initiatives to ensure that young infants receive the care and nurturing they need in the first six years of life, so that their brains can develop to their full potential. Governments in North America have been extremely slow to act on these calls.

The only negative consequence of the new research is that people could easily conclude that, if you fail to change an infant's brain in the first six years of life, you have missed the window of opportunity. People who acknowledge that the brain is malleable in the early years sometimes adopt a fatalistic view of children who have not been lucky enough to have been nurtured in their infancy. But this view, like the view that our fate is determined by our genetic make-up, is based on science that is increasingly out of date.

In the late 1980s neurologists began to see evidence that the adult brain is more plastic than they had previously suspected. They found, for instance, that new areas of the brain could be activated and rewired to compensate for damaged parts affected by a stroke, and that the brains of adults who take up the violin, even after the age of forty, show significant development and reorganization. In his book *The Mind and the Brain,* neurologist Jeffrey Schwartz gives a picture of how far our understanding of the brain has come:

> A mere twenty years ago neuroscientists thought that the brain was structurally immutable by early childhood and that its functions and abilities were programmed by genes. We now know that this is not so. To the contrary: the brain's ensembles of neurons change over time, forming new connections that become stronger with use, and letting unused synapses weaken until they are able to carry signals no better than a frayed string between two tin cans in

the old game of telephone. The neurons that pack our brains at the moment of birth continue to weave themselves into circuits throughout our lives. The real estate that the brain devotes to this activity rather than that one, to this part of the body rather than that one, even to this mental habit rather than that one, is as mutable as a map of congressional districts in the hands of gerrymanders. The life we lead, in other words, leaves its mark in the form of enduring changes in the complex circuitry of the brain— footprints of the experiences we have had, and the reactions we have taken. This is neuroplasticity.

One of the most striking discoveries in neuroplasticity, which I believe is connected to the changes I have seen in the children I've taught, was made by Edward Taub in experiments with stroke patients in the 1980s. Before his experiments, physicians thought that "whatever function a patient has regained one year after stroke is all he ever will: his range of motion will not improve for the rest of his life." Taub was convinced that people who suffered from strokes were unable to recover function in the affected limbs because they only ever used the unaffected limbs after the stroke, and the brain modified itself to compensate. He developed a routine called constraint-induced movement therapy, in which stroke patients would wear a sling on their good arm for 90 percent of their waking hours. For six hours a day they would work at using their affected limb, eating lunch, pushing brooms, throwing balls and practising their skills on dexterity boards and pegboards. After only two weeks of CI therapy many patients regained significant use of a limb that they thought would "forever hang uselessly at their side."

When I first read about the way physical abilities quickly emerged in Taub's patients through repetitive exercises, I was reminded of how intellectual abilities have emerged in my students through exercises that involve repeating a great many small steps. I was particularly reminded of some of the changes I saw with Matthew.

In Grade 4 students are expected to be able to move various shapes around on a grid. For instance, they might be asked to slide a shape like the one shown below two units left and three units down.

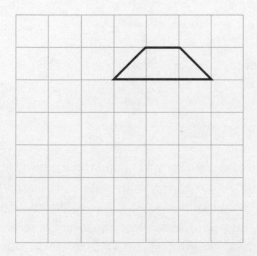

When I first introduced Matthew to grids, I wasn't sure how I could ever teach him to slide a complex shape such as the trapezoid on the previous page; he wasn't able to correctly copy any shape much more complicated than a rectangle. I decided to start with the simplest shape I could think of—a dot. I drew two dots on a grid at the same level and showed Matthew how to find the distance between them by counting the number of steps he would have to take on the grid to get from one dot to the other.

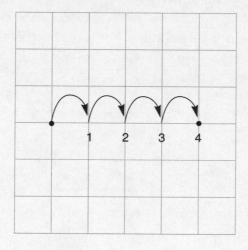

After Matthew had learned to find the distance between a pair of dots, counting both to the right and left and up and down, I showed him how to slide dots on the grid. To slide a dot three units left, he would count over three units and draw a new dot. Eventually he was able to a slide a dot in any combination of directions.

I had planned to teach Matthew to slide a shape by first drawing a dot on one of the corners of the shape, then moving the dot and then the shape. I shaded a square on the grid and drew a dot on one corner. I asked Matthew to slide the dot three units to the right and then draw a copy of the square as if it had moved along with the dot. I was surprised at the result: he slid the dot correctly, but when he tried to slide the square he drew it in the wrong position.

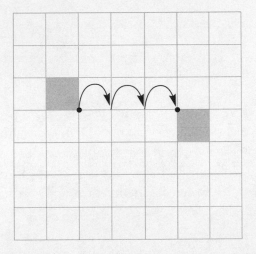

I tried to explain to Matthew how to position the square relative to the dot ("Look, the square is to the left of the dot and above it"), but no matter how many explanations I supplied and how much practice I gave him, he still drew the square—apparently at random—in any of the four boxes adjacent to the dot.

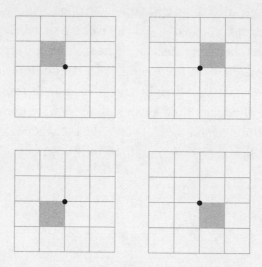

After several lessons I was close to giving up. Then I realized that I could make the problem easier by isolating the two areas of the grid that Matthew needed to compare when he was copying the square. I drew a pair of two-by-two grids, each with a dot in its centre, and shaded a square in one of the grids.

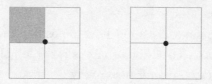

I asked Matthew to copy the shaded square in the first grid so that it was in the same position in the second grid. Matthew was able to use the border of the first grid to help him see where the square was relative to the dot. He had no trouble copying the square so that it was in the same position in the second grid. I then drew grids with squares in each of the four possible positions, and Matthew was soon able to copy the square when it was in any position. I began increasing the size of the two grids (starting with a three-by-three grid) until the grids merged and Matthew was able to slide the square on a continuous grid. I also increased the complexity of the shape he had to copy, and after a few lessons he was able to successfully slide a shape like the one shown above.

The work of neurologists such as Taub has shown that cognitive function can be built even when there appears to be no physical basis in the brain for that function. When a therapist takes a paralyzed limb and guides it through the motions of a healthy limb, the limb can come to life, even when it has been paralyzed for years. I have seen something similar happen with children learning mathematics, even those whose brains seemed to be damaged or dormant in some way. When those children were taken through the motions of doing mathematics, even when there seemed to be no hope that their brains could ever work properly, conceptual abilities emerged.

One of the great mistakes we make with children who are challenged is to start at too high a level and not to work back and forth between different levels of abstraction. Recently I had an opportunity to work with a Grade 3 student who couldn't add and who couldn't even tell me how many fingers he had raised when I helped him hold up three fingers.

However, the boy could count, so I decided to see what I could build up from this starting point. I wrote

$$6 + 1$$

I asked him to say "six" with his fist closed. Then I asked him to say the number that comes after six while raising one of his fingers. The boy said "seven" and raised his thumb. I told him that the number he said when he raised his thumb was the answer: he had successfully added 6 + 1. The boy was very happy to hear this.

After he had used the same method to add one to several other one-digit numbers, I began to raise the bar, exactly as I had done with Matthew. The secret of raising the bar is to make questions look harder without increasing the level of difficulty or introducing new skills or information until the student has consolidated the step you want to teach. I asked the boy to add one to larger and larger numbers: 17 + 1, 23 + 1, 35 + 1 and so on. When I reached 93 + 1, the boy was as excited as Matthew had been when he added the fractions with the huge denominators.

I then showed the boy how to add the number two to a given number by raising two fingers as he counted up from the number. Before long the boy could add three to any number, even though he hadn't previously been able to recognize three fingers. I'm certain he could have moved on to adding four or five if we hadn't run out of time. Our lesson ended with him running around the class proudly showing off his work to the teacher and the other students. I have taught many students to understand addition from this simple starting point.

You may have noticed that the trick I used to raise the bar for the Grade 3 student and the one I used with Matthew when he was adding fractions are virtually identical. In both cases I made the questions look harder by making the numbers that didn't play much of a role in the calculation (the denominator of the fraction, the number added to one) larger and larger. In math it is always easy to find a way to raise the bar and get a student excited. But when we teach elementary students who are challenged, we often refuse to stoop to something so easy, because we think mathematical concepts have to be hard.

The method of building ability in steps by incrementally raising the bar can be used to teach problem solving as well as operations. A year ago I began trying to teach Matthew some basic problem solving skills. Because Matthew still got very nervous when he encountered new material, especially when he couldn't see what to do right away, I decided to give him some problems that might have more than one answer, where he would have to search among different possibilities, using trial and error to find a solution. I wanted to help Matthew develop mental stamina by having him solve problems that require persistence.

One of the problems I gave Matthew required placing three pennies on a diagram like the one below so that either an odd or even number of pennies was in each shape.

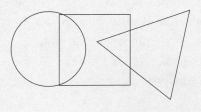

For instance, you might try to place an odd number of pennies in the circle, an even number in the triangle and an even number in the square, or an odd number of pennies in the circle, an odd number in the triangle and an odd number in the square and so on. (The trick is to place the right number of pennies in the overlapping parts of the figures.)

When I gave Matthew the three pennies he clearly had no idea how to approach the problem. He was so nervous at first that he would place the pennies in the shapes without looking, and then announce that he had found the solution. This kind of reaction will be familiar to anyone who has taught a child having difficulty in math. Most children who have struggled with math for years will develop a kind of guessing mechanism that usually serves them well at school. No matter what you are teaching, even if it is quite simple, they often don't have a clue what you are saying. They will try to get a vague sense of your meaning, but most of their attention is diverted to formulating a good guess. When I first start teaching these students, much of the work is designed to break such habits.

To help Matthew learn to work more systematically, I decided to simplify the problem. I drew a pair of figures—an overlapping circle and a triangle—and asked him to place an odd number of pennies in the circle and an even number in the triangle. But he still insisted on guessing a solution at random. So I drew a circle, placed a small number of pennies inside it and asked him to simply count the pennies and say whether there was an even or odd number in the circle. When he could tell me the answer without counting, I placed some pennies in the overlapping circle and triangle and asked him to describe what he saw. Then I started writing statements that described the arrangement, such as "There is an odd number in the circle and an even number in the triangle." I would ask Matthew to tell me if each statement was true or false. To prevent him from guessing I asked him to go through the steps of his thinking out loud. For example, he would say, "There are two pennies in the circle and that's even. So it's false that there is an odd number of pennies in the circle." I then wrote some mock tests in which I had purposely made some mistakes. I asked Matthew to mark the tests and point out my mistakes (he took great pleasure in this) and to give me a mark. Finally, when he could consistently catch my errors, I had him solve a number of puzzles involving two shapes.

After several lessons of this sort I felt Matthew was finally ready to tackle the problem with three shapes. At first he found the problem very difficult and I had to give him hints, but after a few tries he suddenly started finding the solutions consistently without my help. Quite often he could see where to place the coins after only a moment's thought and sometimes he was able to find different solutions for the same problem. The sudden emergence of this ability was quite striking, as though a limb that had been dragged through a series of repetitive motions had suddenly started to move gracefully on its own.

Breaking concepts and skills into steps is often necessary even with more able students. Math is a subject in which a gifted student can become a struggling student almost overnight, because mathematical knowledge is cumulative.

If a student misses a step in math it is often hard to go on. That is why it is so important for the teacher to know how to break mathematical concepts into steps.

I have taught math to many students who struggled in the subject but who did not appear to have any real learning disabilities or challenges. Using the methods I describe in this book, I have always found it extremely easy to teach these students. But I have also managed to teach mathematics to students who I thought initially would never learn the subject. Matthew and Lisa didn't know any number facts and couldn't make the most elementary inferences when I started teaching them—they appeared to have no mental foundation on which I could build. But Lisa eventually went into academic math, and Matthew is now developing a real sense of numbers.

Not long ago I started teaching a nine-year-old girl who appeared to have no working memory. She had suffered brain damage at birth and consequently had enormous difficulty retaining facts, particularly in mathematics. It took about six lessons before she could consistently count the shaded pieces in a fraction or remember which number goes on top and which goes on the bottom. Sometimes she would even forget how many pieces she had counted when she went to write the number down. I had never seen a student who had so much trouble naming fractions.

In our sixth lesson she did something that surprised me. I had drawn a pie cut into four pieces and shaded three of the pieces. She counted the shaded pieces and wrote the number three as the numerator of the fraction. Then, rather than counting the pieces all over again, as she always did to find the denominator of the fraction, she simply counted the remaining piece in the fraction as four. She remembered that she had already counted three pieces and deduced, without any help from me, that she could count on from where she had stopped to find the total number of pieces in the pie. This might seem like an inconsequential step, but given the difficulty I had getting her to remember how to name a fraction or even which pieces she had counted, what she did seemed almost uncanny. Since then new abilities of this kind have emerged consistently in our lessons. After about twenty lessons she can now hold in her head two or three steps of an operation or process at once, and she generally learns three or four new things in a lesson.

In teaching children who appear to be incapable of learning mathematics, I believe we make the same mistake that doctors made for years with stroke patients. We can't imagine being able to break through the blank stares of these children any more than we would hope for a stroke patient's lifeless limb to gain mobility. We assume that nothing is to be gained by putting their minds and hands through the motions of calculating and manipulating symbols, because they seem to lack the spark of intelligence that would invest these activities with life and meaning.

Traditional models of learning assume that intelligence and mathematical ability are fixed and that reducing explanations to small steps can add only tiny increments to a student's knowledge. Slower children may become a little better at math, but only by parroting what they have learned by rote. But this way of looking at intelligence does not take account of the way complex systems such as the brain actually behave; in such systems a series of small changes can have dramatic effects.

Scientists have recently taken to studying ant colonies to help them understand how groups of neurons, which are not themselves intelligent or sentient, can act collectively to produce intelligent behaviour. Computer scientists have even used the insights they gained from ant colonies to design expert systems. Ants communicate by using scent chemicals that they secrete along trails or exchange by touching antennae. The overall behaviour of an ant colony emerges from a multitude of individual chemical exchanges that are not in themselves directed by any central authority. The individual agents in the colony, working at one scale— by passing on and reacting to chemical signals—produce collective behaviour that appears to have a sense of purpose when looked at on a larger scale. Ant colonies have a memory and can learn to solve problems through experience. They can even find optimal solutions to complex geometric problems such as finding the exact spot to leave their dead—at a maximum distance from all of the nests.

The large-scale behaviours of complex systems are extremely sensitive to small changes of condition. The arrival in a nest of the right number of patrol ants at the right frequency can cause the forager ants to leave the nest en masse in search of food. Minute changes in humidity or temperature, in the amount of waste in the colony or in the number of foreign ants encountered can cause the colony to move, to reorganize itself into larger or smaller nests or to attack another colony.

Scientists who study complexity have coined the phrase "more is different" to describe the way tiny perturbations in a complex system can cascade, or add up, to produce non-linear effects. A sequence of small inputs will not necessarily produce a little more or less of a particular quality of the system. In fact, new properties may emerge that seem greater than or different from the sum of the parts of the system. These emergent properties cannot easily be reduced or traced to the actions of the various components of the system.

Like the chemical solution that changes colour with the addition of a single drop of reagent or the ant colony that begins to forage for food with the arrival of a few ants, the brain can acquire new abilities that emerge suddenly and dramatically from a series of small conceptual advances. I have witnessed the same progression in hundreds of students: a surprising leap forward, followed by a period where the student appears to have reached the limits of his or her ability, then a tiny advance that precipitates another leap. This phenomenon, which I call emergent intelligence, has not been taken account of in education. Our schools are still based on rigid hierarchies of talent and intelligence, the product of outmoded views of the brain and of complex systems in general.

A growing body of evidence in the study of cognition now shows that the vast majority of children are born with the ability to learn anything and that the brain is plastic until much later in life than scientists previously believed. As well, other evidence, which I will discuss in the next chapter, suggests that with proper instruction, abilities can be developed in any subject.

Many people still believe that children are born with vastly different mental abilities and that there is little a teacher or parent can do for a child who is born without ability. When I wrote *The Myth of Ability* I thought that this belief was the main impediment to nurturing emergent intelligence in children in our society. However, in my work in the school system for the past five years, I have observed other barriers to nurturing ability that are at least as detrimental to education as the myth that ability is inborn. Some of those barriers lie in current educational theory, some in current teaching practice and some in larger, systemic problems in the school system.

CHAPTER THREE

MISTAKING THE ENDS FOR THE MEANS IN EDUCATION

IT'S HARD TO IMAGINE why anyone would want to compare the game of chess to a fruit fly, but scientists have recently taken to calling chess "the *Drosophila* of cognitive science." Like the lowly fruit fly, whose life cycle is measured in weeks and whose chromosomes are marked with bar codes of light and dark bands that make them particularly easy to read, chess has been the subject of an inordinate number of scientific papers.

There are several reasons why a game in which two players move an odd assortment of religious and military figures around sixty-four squares has become "the greatest single test bed for theories of thinking." On one hand, measurement of chess skill has now advanced to a point where players' ratings predict the outcomes of games with remarkable reliability. On the other hand, chess is widely considered to be, in the words of the poet Goethe, a "touchstone of intelligence." Relying on uncanny powers of intuition and creativity, grandmasters have defeated dozens of less talented opponents in simultaneous games, even when they were allowed only seconds to glance at the board between moves.

In "The Expert Mind," an article that appeared in *Scientific American* in July 2006, Philip Ross examines the implications of a century of research on how experts develop ability in chess and other fields and on how the expert mind processes and retrieves information. His conclusions lend strong support to the notion of emergent intelligence.

> The preponderance of psychological evidence indicates that experts are made not born. What is more, the demonstrated ability to turn a child quickly into an expert—in chess, music and a host of other subjects—sets a clear challenge before the schools. Can educators find ways to encourage students to engage in the kind of effortful study that will improve their reading and math skills? . . . Instead of perpetually pondering the question, "Why can't Johnny read?" perhaps educators should ask, "Why should there be anything in the world he can't learn to do?"

Ross's article confirms what good teachers tend to know: that through effortful study children can quickly develop abilities in subjects for which they previously showed no real aptitude or gift. But implicit in "The Expert Mind" is an idea that, in my opinion, has even more profound implications for education.

At first glance the results of the psychological research that Ross cites seem counterintuitive. The point of training to be an expert in any particular game, chess included, is to play the game. But the kind of training in which chess experts engage, which includes playing small sets of moves over and over, memorizing tens of thousands of positions and obsessively studying the techniques of the masters, appears to play a greater role in the development of ability than the actual playing out of a game. That is why, according to Ross,

> it is possible for enthusiasts to spend thousands of hours playing chess or golf or a musical instrument without ever advancing beyond the amateur level and why a properly trained student can overtake them in a relatively short time. It is interesting to note that time spent playing chess, even in tournaments, appears to contribute less than such study to a player's progress; the main training value of such games is to point up weaknesses for future study.

The idea that children or adults who spend a great deal of time playing a game or exploring a subject, either on their own or with a little guidance, will not necessarily become good at the game or subject, whereas a person who is rigorously trained can become an expert in a relatively short time, runs counter to current educational practice.

Most people think that training requires endless boring and mind-numbing repetition. But I argue that schools can give children rigorous training in skills and concepts without putting them through the pain that people associate with rote learning and drills. There are deep psychological truths about children that I feel have been largely overlooked in debates about the curriculum. If I have come to see anything as innate in children, it is the propensity to learn, and to enjoy learning the way experts learn.

Even if the work children needed to do to become experts in a subject could not be made fun and engaging, we would still have to ask if this work is beneficial. Experts clearly love doing the things they are good at. So even if the training required to become an expert is at times onerous, the end result might still be worth the effort.

Over the past twenty years many educational theorists have claimed that if children are allowed to play with concrete materials, such as blocks and Cuisenaire rods and fraction strips, and to explore ideas with the right kind of guidance from a teacher, they can turn themselves into experts in mathematics. According to this view, effective teachers can create conditions in their classrooms that will allow their students to construct knowledge and make discoveries, either on their own or with the help of their peers. Teachers shouldn't put too much emphasis on specific knowledge or skills in any subject, nor should they fill up a student's head with facts. The content of a subject is not as important as the way students learn to learn the subject. A famous saying in education, which I have heard several math consultants repeat, captures this philosophy: "The teacher should be the guide on the side, not the sage on the stage." This approach to teaching, which usually goes by the name discovery-based learning or inquiry-based learning, is now mandated in one form or another in curricula across Canada and the United States.

None of the ideas behind discovery-based learning are unreasonable in themselves. I believe very strongly, for instance, that teachers should allow students to discover things independently whenever they can. The teaching methods used in JUMP have been characterized by some educators as rote learning, perhaps because I recommend that teachers guide weaker students in small steps until they have developed the skills and confidence to do more independent work. But, as I will explain later, I always encourage students to take the steps themselves, and as much as possible help them understand why they took each step. This method of teaching, which I call guided discovery, is very different from rote learning. Even when students are capable of taking only the smallest steps, they are still actively involved in making discoveries and constructing their knowledge of mathematics, and are therefore led to understand math at a deeper conceptual level. As students gain confidence through their successes and as they become more engaged in their work, I encourage them to take larger steps and to work more independently.

I believe that the methods I present in this book, which include techniques that Ross identifies as effective at producing experts, are more likely to create students who are motivated to explore ideas and actually make discoveries than the methods used in so-called discovery-based programs. Guiding students to learn and discover things requires an enormous amount of attention to detail, especially if the students have special needs or challenges. A teacher can't simply hand out base-ten blocks and expect the students to discover efficient means for adding and subtracting large numbers. Students need to acquire basic conceptual skills before they can begin to make discoveries, and if they don't manage to discover those skills, they need to be taught them. Good teaching, even by the discovery method, requires constant monitoring, assessment and intervention. The prevailing idea that kids will discover things on their own without careful guidance has prevented us from appreciating the degree of rigour that good teaching requires.

To understand the extent to which schools fail to give students rigorous training, it helps to consider an example. Many high-school teachers complain that their Grade 9 students lack basic skills in areas such as grammar, composition and arithmetic. The tasks of learning the various rules involved in grammar and arithmetic and of memorizing times tables and tenses appear to be beyond many students. But the research in cognition that Ross cites has shown that, with proper training, people can learn far more difficult skills and concepts. I have found, for example, that multiplication facts and standard methods of addition and subtraction (using borrowing or regrouping), long division and long multiplication, as well as operations with decimals and fractions, are extremely easy to teach. Here are several strategies for teaching times tables that show how easy they are to teach.

In one lesson I have taught many Grade 4, 5 and 6 classes how to multiply by the number nine simply by encouraging kids to look closely at the patterns in the nine-times table. I start by writing the first five multiples of nine in a column:

09
18
27
36
45

I ask the class if they can see a pattern in the numbers in the right-hand (the ones) column or the left-hand (the tens) column. Children immediately see that the numbers in the right-hand column decrease by one as you move downwards and the numbers in the left-hand column increase by one. Once the students have seen this pattern, I ask them to use it to extend the chart to ninety.

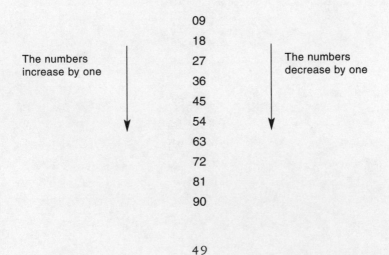

The numbers increase by one

09
18
27
36
45
54
63
72
81
90

The numbers decrease by one

I encourage the children to look for other patterns in the table as well. Many students recognize a kind of symmetry in the chart: each of the first five numbers has a twin with reversed digits in the second half of the table. For instance, 09 has the twin 90, 18 has the twin 81 and so on. Many students also see that if you add the ones digit and the tens digit of any number in the table the result is always nine: $0 + 9 = 9$; $1 + 8 = 9$; $2 + 7 = 9$ and so on. It is not hard to see why this pattern exists: if you add the digits of the first number in the chart $(0 + 9)$, you get a sum of nine. The next number on the chart, 18, has a ones digit that is one less than nine and a tens digit that is one more than zero. Therefore the sum of the digits of eighteen should be the same as the sum of the digits of 09. This pattern continues as you move down the table.

Once students have explored the patterns in the table I fill in the various products of nine:

$$9 \times 1 = 09$$
$$9 \times 2 = 18$$
$$9 \times 3 = 27$$
$$9 \times 4 = 36$$
$$9 \times 5 = 45$$
$$9 \times 6 = 54$$
$$9 \times 7 = 63$$
$$9 \times 8 = 72$$
$$9 \times 9 = 81$$
$$9 \times 10 = 90$$

I ask students to look at the tens digit of each number in the right-hand column and compare it to the number (in bold) on the other side of the equal sign that is multiplied by nine:

$$9 \times 1 = 09$$
$$9 \times 2 = 18$$
$$9 \times 3 = 27$$
$$9 \times 4 = 36$$
$$9 \times 5 = 45$$
$$9 \times 6 = 54$$
$$9 \times 7 = 63$$
$$9 \times 8 = 72$$
$$9 \times 9 = 81$$
$$9 \times 10 = 90$$

Students immediately see that the tens digit of the number to the right of the equal sign is always one less than the number to the left of the equal sign. For instance, the product of 9 x 3 is 27; the tens digit of twenty-seven is two, which is one less than three. Hence it is extremely easy to find the tens digit of any product of nine: just subtract one from the number that you want to multiply by nine. By this reasoning, the tens digit of 9 x 7 must be six, the tens digit of 9 x 9 must be eight, the tens digit of 9 x 4 must be three and so on.

Once students have discovered how to find the tens digit of a product of nine, I immediately give them a test on this one skill so that they can all show off what they have learned, and so they consolidate their knowledge of this particular skill before I teach them any new facts. I write the nine-times table on the board (out of order) and tell the students that to receive full marks on the test they only have to copy out the test and fill in the tens digit of the product.

$$9 \times 7 = \underline{\ }\ \underline{\ } \quad \longrightarrow \quad 9 \times 7 = \underline{6}\ \underline{\ }$$
$$9 \times 4 = \underline{\ }\ \underline{\ } \quad \longrightarrow \quad 9 \times 4 = \underline{3}\ \underline{\ }$$
$$9 \times 8 = \underline{\ }\ \underline{\ } \quad \longrightarrow \quad 9 \times 8 = \underline{7}\ \underline{\ }$$

(and so on)

When everyone has perfected this test I ask the students how they think they could find the missing ones digit in each of their answers. If they need a hint I remind them of what they already know: that the sum of the digits of a product of nine is nine, so they can find the missing ones digit by subtracting the tens digit from nine. For instance, the tens digit of 9×6 is five, and since the digits of 9×6 must add up to nine, the missing ones digit is four; hence $9 \times 6 = 54$. I ask students to fill in the missing numbers on their test by subtracting the tens digit in each of their answers from nine.

This procedure for teaching the nine-times table can be used to teach it to a Grade 4 class in about half an hour. Not all students in a class will necessarily know how to readily subtract a one-digit number from nine (I've found I can't assume this even in Grade 4), so I always spend a few minutes at the beginning of the lesson showing students how they can subtract numbers by counting on their fingers. (For instance, to subtract five from nine, you can say "five" with your fist closed, then count up to nine raising one finger at a time; the number of fingers you have raised is the answer.) I always have some bonus questions on hand for faster students so I have time to make sure that weaker students all get perfect marks on their tests. Some students will need to review the lesson, but with a few minutes of practice every day even weaker students can learn their nine-times table very quickly.

There are many strategies and other patterns in the times tables that a teacher can use to help students remember their tables. Multiplication is a short form of addition: six times three means "add three six times." So a student can always find six times three by first finding five times three and then adding an extra three to the result. Similarly, six times four can be worked out by finding five times four and adding an extra four to the result and so on. Most students know their five-times table by Grade 5, but many do not know their six-times table. Students can learn to multiply a number by six by first multiplying it by five and then adding the number itself to the result (with the proviso that students should eventually memorize the six-times table).

Using patterns and strategies such as the ones I have outlined above, I can teach a Grade 4 or 5 class in a matter of weeks to multiply all pairs of one-digit numbers without a calculator. And, using the strategies I will outline in later chapters, in a matter of months I can teach a Grade 4 or 5 class all of the basic arithmetic operations, such as adding and subtracting multi-digit numbers (with regrouping or borrowing) and long multiplication and division, as well as operations with decimals and fractions.

Some educators assume that students who don't know their times tables or operations can still learn mathematics, as long as they can find the information they need on a calculator or computer. In many schools teachers now spend much more time teaching general concepts and methods for finding mathematical information with calculators and computers than they spend teaching specific facts or procedures. A person who doesn't know how to locate the notes on an instrument can't play music, let alone compose symphonies. People rarely make the mistake of thinking that basic knowledge and skills aren't important in music, probably because the only thing an untrained musician can produce from an instrument is noise. Mathematics, writing and reading, however, are so much part of our daily lives that kids usually pick up some basic skills at home or in public, so they can usually produce something that looks like reading, writing or arithmetic even if they were never taught any basic skills at school. This state of affairs has kept us from seeing the need for rigorous training in these subjects. The basic skills kids happen to pick up outside of school are, unfortunately, not usually sufficient to guarantee success at school.

It is a serious mistake to think that students who don't know number facts can get by in mathematics by using a calculator or other aids. Students can certainly perform operations and produce numbers on a calculator, but if they don't have a sense of numbers, they will not be able to tell if their answers are correct, nor can they develop a talent for solving mathematical problems. To solve problems, students must be able to see patterns in numbers and make estimates and predictions about numbers. A calculator cannot provide those abilities. Trying to do mathematics without knowing basic number facts is like trying to play the piano without knowing where the notes are.

In the debate about whether students should be taught basic skills, a deeper issue has not received enough attention. It is not hard to see that a person needs some knowledge of the basic content of a subject in order to solve problems in that subject. But it is possible that the process of learning the content of a subject can also create mental capacities that are important to conceptual thought—even if the student forgets the details entirely.

One source of confusion around the role of training in education lies in the vast difference between the things people do to become experts and the things they do when they are experts. Experts develop the skills and characteristics that we look for in outstanding students: they love what they do almost to the point of addiction, they are self-motivated and creative, and—in their field—they can see and remember details that elude the untrained eye and solve problems that defeat the amateur. But these abilities often develop from activities that appear to have little in common with true expertise. It seems inconceivable that anything original or inspiring could originate in things that are themselves mechanical or derivative, but the abilities of experts often emerge from exercises that involve a great deal of practice and copying of the styles and ideas of others.

When I was a teenager I desperately wanted to write short stories and poems, but I had trouble producing one tolerable sentence after several hours of work and I could never seem to find anything interesting to write about. After receiving the lowest mark in my creative writing class at university, I doubted that I would ever write anything that could be published. Like most university students, my critical abilities were much more highly developed than my creative ones.

Shortly after I received my undergraduate degree I read a book of letters from the poet Sylvia Plath to her mother. The book was a revelation to me, because it showed quite clearly that Plath managed to teach herself to write through sheer determination. As a teenager she had practised, with a relentless will, the literary equivalent of the training that produces grandmasters: she learned everything she could about poetic metre and form, she read widely in mythology, she studied other poets obsessively and she memorized a thesaurus. She also did something that we would never tell young writers to do now, but that probably contributed the most to developing her talent: she wrote imitations of the poems she loved. Plath's early poems were extremely derivative, but gradually, as she developed her craft, her own voice began to appear. Eventually she became one of the most original poets of the past century.

Reading about the methods that Plath used to teach herself to write gave me a great deal of hope. For the first time in my life I saw a path I could follow towards developing a skill in something. I still remember the day, two years after

I had started slavishly imitating the work of Plath and other writers, when I first saw a trace of my own voice in a poem I had written. And later I started the whole process of imitation all over again to learn how to write plays.

When I started having some success with my plays, I realized that I hadn't known how to observe the world until I had learned some measure of craft. I couldn't know which of my experiences were dramatic, or which things I had heard people say would be interesting or funny on stage, until I had spent a great deal of time learning the literary forms that my experiences would fit into. We tend to think that children will just look at the world and interesting stories and observations will pour out of them naturally. This sometimes does happen, and teachers should certainly encourage their students to write even when they don't have any technical skills. But children can be helped to create and to feel that they don't have to invent a style from scratch if they are taught about the formal tools that writers can use to convey their ideas.

Once I taught some high-school students to write poetry by using the following method. I taught them what metaphors and similes were and then I gave each student a book of contemporary poetry. I asked the students to write down the beginning of a metaphor or a simile—for example, "The moon was like . . ." or "The water is . . ."—and then I told them to open their book of poetry and find a phrase that could complete the metaphor or simile. After the students had created a page of metaphors and similes, I asked them to select the ones that made sense and that they liked and to put them next to each other to see if they

inspired any ideas. I also asked them to write lines they
thought might fill in the gaps between the similes and
metaphors they had created. Here are some excerpts from
the poems they created:

> A lipstick stain lightly decorates the collar of his shirt
> like the silhouette of a butterfly dancing.
> An expendable souvenir to be laundered into obscurity.

> Your nest in the corner of the ceiling made by the
> music of the radio, lined in cottony static. I loved your
> eyrie up there, held in place with cobwebs and static.
> Your throat an aqueduct in a sunny country. Ink in
> our blood that year, living story.

> The water felt like spring rain
> My life, my death, desolate pain
> Fear death by water; promises in vain

> Poetry as wild as the Dakotan tumbleweed.
> No connection, free to whims and wind
> Free to imagination and will
> Free to choose and not to choose.

> You leave for the hills that are
> hiding your purpose
> The numberless slaughtered
> scattered like fallen walls of the empire.

> My solitude was like a small bell. I kept it close to me
> and rang it often. When I first talked to him, he told
> me he was coming home, and his voice across the line
> sounded like a stream, tripping over his word stones.

Many of the students said they found the exercise very helpful and that it made them feel as if they were capable of writing. The rules of the exercise gave them a starting point so they didn't have to create a poem from scratch. Using the found phrases in the book and placing the lines they had created next to each other helped to spark their imaginations.

The abilities of some artists and scientists seem to develop out of nowhere. Because complex systems such as the brain display emergent behaviour, it is not surprising that extraordinary abilities will appear in some children at an early age. Ross speculates that prodigies such as Wolfgang Amadeus Mozart, who wrote his first compositions when he was five years old, and Carl Friedrich Gauss, whose contribution to the field of mathematics is immense, somehow managed to train themselves when they were very young, perhaps because they had developed an obsessive interest in the things they did well. Gauss used to help his father with his accounts when he was three and Mozart learned to play the piano at a similarly early age. But even if the abilities of prodigies happen to spring from a mysterious genetic or otherworldly source, this doesn't imply that we can't train abilities in children who are not prodigies. As Ross points out, exceptional ability can certainly be trained in chess; a Hungarian chess enthusiast once set out to train all three of his daughters to be grandmasters, and he succeeded.

In talking to various artists and scientists or reading their biographies, I've found that people who have actually made scientific discoveries or created works of art (as opposed to people who theorize about these things) tend to acknowledge the role of practice in their work. Writers and artists, for instance, know from experience how many years of studies and student exercises it can take before they find their voice or style. Ernest Hemingway, who eventually achieved a remarkable economy of style, as a young writer set himself the task of producing one decent sentence per day, and Paul Klee, whose mature paintings are imbued with a profound sense of mystery, spent ten formative years painting tonal exercises that would help him understand colour. Scientists and mathematicians in particular understand how much time they must devote to learning basic skills—as well as everything previously discovered in their area of specialization—before they can do original work. It is no accident that parents and academics who have a background in these fields have led the campaign for more rigorous standards in schools.

When so many experts acknowledge the importance of training in the development of talent, and when so much evidence in cognition suggests that experts can be trained, why are schools so reluctant to expose children to anything that looks like rigorous training? The answer lies in a philosophy that has its roots in the ideas of Jean-Jacques Rousseau and

John Dewey, and more recently in the psychological theories of Jean Piaget and Lev Vygotsky. Known as constructivism, it has had a profound influence in our schools, particularly in the past two decades.

As an educational philosophy, constructivism is not easy to define. Without stretching its basic principles too far, one can make the case that almost any educational program is constructivist. Looked at with a subtle eye, even JUMP could be seen as constructivist. I will, in fact, argue that the teaching methods used in JUMP are consistent with some of the most important insights of constructivism. However, as an educational method, constructivism has failed to live up to its promise, because its foundational ideas, as well as those of associated philosophies that underlie discovery-based learning, have been misapplied, owing to confusions that are in essence confusions about language. I believe that JUMP has the potential to fulfill many of the constructivist movement's aims, although in a manner somewhat different from that advocated by its leading proponents.

One of the central ideas of constructivism is that "only constructed knowledge—knowledge which one finds out for oneself—is truly integrated and understood." Many educators who espouse constructivist ideas claim that subjects such as math and science are better learned by doing than by more passive methods such as listening to a teacher. According to this view, teachers should immerse students in environments that are both rich and real, and students should be encouraged to develop their own ideas rather than being told answers or memorizing them. Some ideas usually associated with educational constructivism are that concepts should be emphasized over procedures, parts should be understood in the context of the whole, and kids should be taught the big picture or the big ideas rather than a collection of steps or procedures for finding answers.

I have a great deal of sympathy for constructivism, and I think that any successful educational program must incorporate some constructivist ideas. Educational constructivism has taken hold in our schools partly as a reaction to rote learning. Too often in the math wars we tend to throw out the good with the bad and we swing wildly back and forth between competing trends. So it is important to understand both the strengths and weaknesses of constructivism.

The philosopher John Dewey, one of the forerunners of constructivism, wrote eloquently about the need to change the teaching methods that were in use at the end of the nineteenth century. Dewey saw that the rigid school system of the day was stifling students. Sitting at desks for hours copying down facts, children were being forced " . . . into the role of passive receptacles, waiting to have information instilled instead of allowing them to move about, discuss, experiment, work on communal projects, pursue research activities in the field and outdoors or indoors in the library or laboratory." You can see how much Dewey's ideas have taken hold in the schools of today, with many positive effects: schools now recognize that children can learn in many ways besides sitting in desks listening to lectures or regurgitating facts they have memorized. But, like every corrective idea, this approach needs to be applied with a sense of balance.

JUMP has been heavily criticized by some math consultants and educational experts who espouse constructivist ideas. These experts generally like to call programs that conform to their philosophy "conceptual" and everything else "non-conceptual." A teacher who had great success with the JUMP program once wrote to a math consultant at her school board to see if she was at all interested in hearing about her experiences. The consultant wrote back to say that the board wasn't interested, because "at a time when the push is for conceptual understanding, JUMP goes against the grain to some degree."

As a mathematician I thought that I understood math "conceptually." And I thought I knew how to teach math reasonably well. I have, after all, taken a number of remedial students into the academic stream and helped many more failing students to do well in math. I have also taught numerous gifted students, right up to a graduate level. The more I thought about the way JUMP had been branded as non-conceptual, the more I realized that this description was based on misuse of language. I believe that some educators have been so seduced by the language they use that they can't clearly see the issues anymore.

Wittgenstein believed that people who philosophize or create theories in the social sciences keep making the same kinds of logical and linguistic mistakes over and over. At the heart of our problems in education is a constant misuse of language of the sort that Wittgenstein identified in philosophy. To see how these confusions have come about, it helps to look at what some educational experts have written about their methods.

Marilyn Burns is a teacher who has written many books that contain some very good mathematical exercises for children. From what I have read of her work, I expect that she is an exceptional teacher. But some of the recommendations she has for teachers can easily be misapplied or misunderstood (as is the case with the ideas I present in this book). She has written, for example, "Set the following expectations for your students: Do only what makes sense to you. Too often students see math as a collection of steps and tricks they must learn. And this misunderstanding leads to common recurring errors." I'm not sure exactly what Burns means when she says, "Do only what makes sense to you." I certainly agree that teachers generally should ask students only to do things that make sense, but I suspect that my understanding of what makes sense to children is much broader than for most educators.

Many educational experts believe that mathematical concepts don't make sense to children unless the teacher starts with the big picture or the big idea. A teacher should always aim to teach students the whole concept, not just a collection of procedures that they will only partially understand. Students should also be shown why the concept is relevant and why they would want to learn it. But this idea, while reasonable, has to be taken with a grain of salt. Anyone who has taught children knows that it is not always practical to start with the big picture, because the human mind can hold only so much information at a time, and an overwhelmed student can shut down or easily be discouraged.

I once observed an intern from teachers' college trying to teach a boy from a Grade 7 special education class how to draw mixed fractions. The boy was getting frustrated, as the intern kept asking him to carry out several steps at a time. I offered to help and asked the boy to simply draw a picture showing the number of whole pies in the fraction 2 1/2. He drew and shaded the pieces in two whole pies. I then asked him to draw the number of whole pies in 3 1/2, 4 1/2 and 5 1/2 pies. He was very excited when he completed the work I had assigned and I could see that he was making more of an effort to concentrate. I asked him to draw the number of whole pies in 2 1/4, 2 3/4, 3 1/4, 4 1/4, then in 2 1/3, 2 1/3, 3 1/3 pies and so on (I started with quarters rather than thirds because they are easier to draw). When the boy could draw the whole number of pies in any mixed fraction, I showed him how to draw the fractional part. Within a few minutes he was able to draw any mixed fraction. If I hadn't broken the skill into two steps (drawing the number of whole pies, then drawing the fractional part) and allowed him to practise each step separately, he might never have learned the concept.

Another problem with the idea that teachers should always start with big ideas is that it leads to confusion over the size of the step a student should be expected to take—just because the step is small doesn't mean the work is not conceptual. As weaker students learn to concentrate and approach their work with real excitement (which generally happens when they start having success), the teacher can begin to skip steps and challenge the students to take larger steps by themselves. In general it might be better to start with big ideas, but only if the students can handle them.

When I teach students to add one to a number by first saying the number with their fist closed and then raising their thumb as they count on to the next number, the concept of addition doesn't suddenly make complete sense to them. They don't know, for instance, that addition commutes (in other words, you can add a pair of numbers in any order) and they couldn't show me with money or base-ten materials how to regroup. But, while they are still very far from understanding addition, by teaching them to add by counting up from a number on their fingers, I am beginning to put the number-line, or the sequence of the numbers, in their body. As well I am giving them a tool that will help them keep up with the other students and a task they can succeed at. And they are beginning to make discoveries on their own. Without telling my students I will often change the order of the numbers in the sums I give them, so that the bigger number comes after the smaller number. Students quickly discover that it is more efficient to start counting up from the larger number, no matter which position it is in. In this way they begin to understand how useful it is that the operation of addition commutes. They begin to see part of the big picture.

Gary Larsen, the cartoonist, once said he found it amusing when his readers complained that he had portrayed a male mosquito sucking blood (only females suck blood), but no one took issue with the fact that the mosquito was wearing clothes and could speak English. The issue of what does and doesn't makes sense to a person is extremely subtle and may depend on many things, including the person's age, experience and culture. The expression "suspension of disbelief" was coined by the poet Coleridge to describe a reader's willingness to accept details of a story that aren't entirely plausible or coherent in return for the promise of entertainment or enlightenment. The same term might be used to describe children's capacity to accept a partial truth, or wait for understanding of the whole to emerge, in return for the teacher's promise that they will have fun and success in their lessons. It is precisely the ability of children to suspend disbelief, or to suspend the need to understand things completely, that gives them such vibrant imaginations and allows them to move through a sequence of incomplete mental models from one level of understanding to the next.

Even with adults, full understanding of a concept rarely emerges without a great deal of effort and practice, and the moment of comprehension is often preceded by long stretches of uncertainty, confusion and incomplete understanding. The great mathematician John Von Neumann once said that learning mathematics is a matter of getting used to things. Children need even more time than adults to get used to things, because they must develop their knowledge of the world and their ability to reason and make inferences. The capacity to suspend disbelief gives children the intellectual fortitude they need to absorb vast amounts of information quickly (without worrying too much about apparent contradictions or the big picture) and to make sense of a world where the Easter Bunny and terrorists coexist and where very little ever seems to make sense.

Unfortunately, children do not have the intellectual fortitude needed to deal with constant failure. Marilyn Burns has
said that "success comes from understanding," but one
might just as well say that understanding comes from success. Success is not simply a by-product of learning, it is the
very foundation of learning. Generally the things that children can do successfully make sense to them, even if they
don't always completely understand what they are doing.
That is why programs that give children too many tasks they
can't perform, or that lose sight of the building blocks to
construct a larger conceptual understanding, are bound to
fail. An author who expects readers to follow the twists and
turns of a complicated story must give them some gratifica-
tion along the way. The details of the story must be engaging
and comprehensible even if the author doesn't give away the
whole plot, or else the reader will soon put the book aside.

Teachers who believe that they must always start with the
big idea will often introduce topics at too high a level for the
majority of students. They will try, for instance, to present concepts such as addition or place value in full generality, in the
context of a rich problem that may require a range of skills or
knowledge to solve, rather than assigning weaker students
tasks they can succeed at, like counting up from a given number on their fingers or identifying the tens digit in a variety of
numbers. Many teachers have been taught that it is a mistake
to start with such basic tasks, that concepts cannot emerge
out of simple, incremental steps because concepts are uni-
fied wholes that are comprehended or imbued with meaning
only in some relevant context. Textbooks and math programs

that are based on this premise—that math will always make sense in the larger context—have actually made math senseless for many students, particularly in schools where parents have neither the time or the ability to help their children with homework nor the financial means to hire a tutor.

Teachers are often afraid that they will bore the faster kids if they try to give weaker students the means to make sense of a lesson by reviewing and practising basic skills and concepts before they move on to the bigger picture. But I have found that there is always a way to entertain faster students, even while starting at the right level for the weaker students, because I can always make the simplest task look a lot harder without going off topic.

I am not advocating that teachers make math a collection of senseless steps and tricks, or that they shouldn't aim to show kids how concepts are relevant and how they are connected to other concepts. But educational theorists must broaden their definition of what makes sense to children. In the educational debates it is not hard to find examples of words that have been defined too narrowly.

I will return to this issue in chapter four, to look at the way terms such as "meaning" and "relevance" have been defined in education, and in chapter seven, to look at the term "concept." Confusion in education sometimes stems from the fallacy of equivocation: educators will use a word that has more than one meaning as if the meaning of the word in one context still holds in a very different context. The most influential educational body in North America, the National Council of Teachers of Mathematics (NCTM),

released a set of standards in the 1990s that largely determined the mathematics curriculum in every school board
in North America and still forms the basis for the present
math curricula in Canada. According to the standards,
"mathematics and science are learned by doing rather than
by passive methods of learning such as watching a teacher
work at the chalk board. Inquiry-based learning and hands-
on learning more effectively engage students than lectures."
This statement trades on the double meaning of passive. A
person who sits still is physically passive, but not necessarily
mentally passive. If watching someone talk is passive, then
listening to a teacher read a story, hearing an author read
from her work or watching a play is also passive.

Clearly children don't have to propel themselves around
the classroom in order to be learning. My best teacher in
high school always had my classmates and me on the edge
of our seats during his chemistry lessons. He led the class in
steps, always giving us enough guidance to deduce the next
step by ourselves. We always felt like we were on the verge of
recreating the discoveries of the great chemists. While it is
of benefit for children to learn by being physically active,
this is not the only way to actively learn.

In the debates over math education one finds all the falla-
cies that practised debaters use to confuse their opponents.
Constructivist ideas have easily carried the day across North
America because the educators who espouse these ideas
have won their arguments by creating false dichotomies,
by using equivocation and by defining their terms too narrowly. After all, what teacher wouldn't want to teach math

conceptually or in a way that makes sense, and what teacher wouldn't want students to be active rather than passive?

Because of confusions over language we have persistently mistaken the ends of education with the means for achieving those ends. We want children to communicate in mathematics, so we fill their texts with so much language that they can't learn the math we expect them to explain. We want them to understand the big ideas, so we teach them the whole concept before they have the skills and knowledge required to understand the parts. We want them to do original work, so we fail to give them the practice or the models they need to be creative. We want them to be resilient, independent problem solvers, so we cause them to struggle and fail so often that they are afraid to attempt anything new.

The idea that teachers should always start with the big idea is particularly damaging when combined with another leading idea in education. Many educators believe that children go through definite stages of cognitive development in mathematics that can be precisely defined and accurately assessed and that must always be taken account of in introducing concepts. A child who can't explain a concept fully or extend the concept to new cases is not developmentally ready to be introduced to the concept, and any effort to introduce children to a concept before they are ready to understand it or the big idea in its entirety (or to discover it on their own) will harm them—or so the theory goes.

The idea that children pass through rigid developmental levels must be approached with caution. We still know very little about the brain. In the past we made a serious mistake by thinking that because the genetic code was rigid, or fixed, in the DNA, a child's development was also rigid and predetermined. We overlooked the epigenome, the interface between the code and its actual expression in a person's characteristics and behaviour. We are in danger of making the same mistake when we assume that children have rigid developmental levels determined by the structure of the brain. The various interfaces between the brain and the environment are at least as complex as the epigenetic system. If we change the environment we may dramatically change the output of the brain, and even the brain itself.

Programs that claim to be able to precisely assess kids' developmental levels in math, or that claim that the developmental levels they have discovered are robust and can predict exactly what a child can and can't do, are almost certainly based on pseudo-science. It is easy to see how current theories of education have led us away from the idea that children will benefit from rigorous instruction or training. If children have fixed stages in their development when they naturally understand ideas, there is no point in training students in increments or small steps; the student will either be ready to understand the concept or not. So the training will either be unnecessary (because the kid will naturally see the whole picture) or unproductive (because the kid will not be developmentally ready).

The idea that children have definite developmental levels and that teachers should always wait until students have reached the appropriate level before they introduce a concept has done inestimable damage in special education classes and to weaker students in general. I have worked with many Grade 6 and 7 students who were held back at a Grade 1 or 2 level in math because their teachers didn't think they were cognitively or developmentally ready to be introduced to the big ideas. Teachers will never foster emergent intelligence or induce the intellectual leaps I have observed unless they are willing to start adding those small drops of knowledge that will cause a student's brain to reorganize itself. If a teacher waits year after year for the student to become developmentally ready to discover or comprehend a concept in its entirety, the student will inevitably become bored and discouraged at being left behind, and the teacher will miss an opportunity to harness the non-linear potential of the brain.

While I advocate that children be given more rigorous instruction and training than they receive at present, it is important that schools not swing back to rote learning. We must take the insights of constructivism to heart: as much as possible, children should be encouraged to discover things on their own, to understand the whole concept and to play at learning. I learned almost as much from playing strategy games in after-school clubs in high school as I did from school itself. I would read the rule books as fast as I could because I wanted to play the games, so I learned how to absorb and synthesize information quickly. Students certainly learn more readily when some reward or goal motivates them.

Schools must weigh the costs and benefits of various approaches to education more carefully than they have done in the past. It might well be more efficient to give kids an enormous amount of practice and training in their early years and then run a more constructivist program in the later years. But an effective balance between guided and independent work should be established by rigorous experimentation, not by theory. I would encourage constructivists to look more closely at JUMP to see if elements of the program might offer a way of meeting their goals. If children were given rigorous guidance in their early years and if they were also encouraged to make discoveries, first in small steps and then in larger and larger steps, schools might well fulfill the constructivist's dream by creating an environment in which children would work the way experts work—for the sheer joy of making discoveries and creating new things.

When I speak about emergent intelligence, I am not referring to the idea of multiple intelligences that Howard Gardner and other psychologists have popularized. The idea that kids have different kinds of intelligence that we should value is very positive. But, unfortunately, some teachers seem to think that kids can have only one type of intelligence—for instance, that they are either kinesthetic or visual spatial learners. I maintain, however, that all of these kinds of intelligence can be trained. Right now the idea of differentiated learning is very popular in our schools, and the idea that teachers should take different approaches with different students is very healthy. But there is a danger that the idea of differentiated instruction, like the idea of developmental levels, will be used as an excuse to leave kids behind. In math it is possible, through rigorous instruction, to teach the whole class roughly the same things at the same time.

The point of giving rigorous instruction to children is not to produce automata who learn simply to please teachers or earn good marks and who never get a chance to play. Kids spend an enormous amount of time at school—far more time than experts spend training. Children could get adequate training and still have lots of time to play. In fact, training can be made into play. Educators often speak as if there are only two possible approaches to education: the constructivist approach, which according to its advocates nurtures deep understanding and engagement in students, and the drills and rote exercises that were once used to turn students into robots. But it is possible to get kids to practise with deep engagement and to guide them in their practice without resorting to rote drills.

The most serious mistake that some educators make is to equate the idea of rigorous instruction with the mistakes of the past—to say we tried training in the past and it didn't work—as if rote learning and drills were the only way to train children. To understand the alternatives we must look more closely at how children learn and, in particular, what motivates them to learn.

—

CHAPTER FOUR

PAYING ATTENTION TO ATTENTION

—

ON A CHILLY FEBRUARY MORNING in 2004 I found myself peering through the bars of a large iron gate in London, England. Beyond the bars I could see the elementary school where I had been invited to teach. The school was surrounded by a high wall, and to get through the gate you had to press a buzzer on an intercom and be admitted by the office. The school was in a very poor neighbourhood, but the level of security seemed excessive.

I spent the morning in meetings with teachers at the school and afterwards ate my lunch in a room that looked down on to the playground. As I watched the students playing during their break, I was shocked by what I saw. Fights had broken out in several parts of the playground and large rings of children had gathered around the fighters to shout encouragement. The adults monitoring the students appeared to have given up hope of controlling them. They would stroll from one fight to another with no apparent sense of urgency, and when they did manage to stop a fight another would immediately break out in its place. In less than ten minutes I saw two children carried off the playground with injuries. I had never seen violence on this scale among elementary students, even in the most difficult schools in Toronto. As I watched the crowds of children fighting and encouraging each other to fight, it struck me how tenuous the order is in any society, and how easily things could fall apart in our cities if the levels of poverty were any higher.

Earlier that morning, when I was still half asleep after my overnight flight from Canada, a teacher had warned me that I would have my work cut out for me at this school. The school administrators had selected thirty of the more difficult and academically challenged students to take part in my demonstration lesson. Fortunately I was to have some help from a teacher and from a local volunteer, Rachel Heywood. Rachel, a city councillor recognized for her charitable work in the community by the mayor of London and the British government, had heard of the JUMP program through a mutual friend and had arranged for me to give three lessons at the school. Even though her expertise wasn't in math education, she had bravely offered to be a volunteer tutor in the class.

At the start of my first lesson I asked the students if they had ever taken apart a computer and seen all the circuits and wires inside. Computers don't have brains made of billions of cells like our brains, so they don't think the way we do. The only thing a computer can do is detect if there is electricity in a particular wire or not. I asked the children how they thought computers could do so many amazing things when they only have this one skill. Then I explained that when computers follow instructions, those instructions are written in a special code. I said I happened to know the code, and I could teach it to them if they would like. But I also warned them that at the end of the lesson I would read their minds by using the code. The students, who were jammed into a very small room, were very excited about this.

Because computers can tell only when there is electricity in a wire and when there is no electricity in a wire, computer codes are generally written with two symbols. When I ask children what number they could use to represent no electricity in a wire, they invariably say "zero," and when I ask them what number might be used to represent electricity in a wire they usually say "one," particularly when I ask them which number besides zero is the easiest to work with. I told the students in my demonstration lesson that the computer codes I was going to show them how to break would be written all in zeroes and ones.

I wrote the number 327 on the board and asked the students to tell me the place value of each of the digits in the number. The number three in 327 actually stands for three hundreds. Because we have ten fingers, our number system is built around multiples of ten, and our place values are ones, tens, hundreds (ten times ten) and thousands (ten times ten times ten). But a computer only has two symbols or states to work with, so it counts by multiples of two— thus it is called a binary system. The place values for a computer are ones, twos, fours (two times two), eights (two times two times two), sixteens and so on (when I showed the students this doubling pattern they continued to find the higher digits).

To a human the number 1011 represents one thousand, no hundreds, one ten and one one, which add up to one thousand and eleven (1000 + 10 + 1). To a computer the number 1011 represents one eight, no fours, one two and a one, which add up to eleven (8 + 2 + 1). So, to a computer the string of symbols 1011 represents the number eleven. To help the students in my demonstration lesson translate between binary codes and regular numbers I asked them to make the following place-value chart:

fours	twos	ones

I knew that dealing with the full binary code would be too difficult for some of the students at first, as most of them were several years below grade level. So rather than having the students write zeroes and ones in the columns, I asked them to copy a sequence of zeroes and checkmarks into the chart.

fours	twos	ones
√	√	0

I told the students to write down the number at the top of any column that had a checkmark in it, and then add the numbers together. In the example above, the fours column and the twos column have checkmarks, so the students would add 4 + 2.

fours	twos	ones
√	√	0

4 + 2 = 6

I wrote up various combinations of checkmarks in the columns, which the students were quite excited to try

fours	twos	ones
√	0	√
0	√	√
0	√	0
√	√	√

4 + 1 = 5
2 + 1 = 3
2 = 2
4 + 2 + 1 = 7

As soon as the students had mastered this step, I wrote exactly the same binary combinations in the chart again, except I used the number in place of a check mark.

fours	twos	ones	
1	0	1	4 + 1 = 5
0	1	1	2 + 1 = 3
0	1	0	2 = 2
1	1	1	4 + 2 + 1 = 7

I told the students that if they treated the symbol 1 like a checkmark, they could translate a number in binary code into a regular number. They quickly decoded the binary numbers I had written on the board, so I then started raising the bar for the class. I asked the students if they could handle bigger numbers (they said, "Yes!"), so I added an eights column to the chart and started writing four-digit numbers in the columns.

eights	fours	twos	ones	
1	0	0	1	8 + 1 = 9
0	1	1	1	4 + 2 + 1 = 7
1	0	1	0	8 + 2 = 10
1	1	0	1	8 + 4 + 1 = 13

I have taught the binary code lesson to several Grade 4 and 5 inner-city classes and I have always been impressed by how excited the students are about breaking the codes. Many classes have asked me to give them binary codes with five or six digits, and students often ask me very deep questions about the codes. One student in an inner-city classroom in Toronto asked how computers are able to represent letters, so I showed the class a simple code for the letters of the alphabet that uses only zeroes and ones. Another student in the same class asked me how I knew that all numbers could be represented by the binary code, so I challenged the class to show me how they could write all the numbers from one to fifteen as sums of the numbers one, two, four and eight, for instance, $9 = 1 + 8$; $11 = 1 + 2 + 8$; $13 = 1 + 4 + 8$; $4 = 4$; $15 = 1 + 2 + 4 + 8$.

In several Grade 4 classes, students who learned how to break numbers into sums of powers of two in this way were able to translate backwards from binary numbers to regular numbers. For example, since $9 = 8 + 1$, nine is one eight, no fours, no twos and one one, so the binary code for nine is 1001. Similarly, since eleven is one eight, no fours, one two and one one, the binary code for eleven is 1011.

After the students in my demonstration lesson were able to translate between binary numbers and regular numbers, I wrote the following charts on the board:

Chart D	Chart C	Chart B	Chart A
8 9 10 11	4 5 6 7	2 3 6 7	1 3 5 7
12 13 14 15	12 13 14 15	10 11 14 15	9 11 13 15

These charts contain all the numbers from one to fifteen organized by how they would be expressed as sums of the numbers 8, 4, 2 and 1 (all of the numbers on Chart D need an 8 in their sum, the numbers on Chart C need a 4 and so on). I asked a volunteer to pick a number between one and fifteen and then tell the number to the class while my back was turned and my ears were plugged (many classes make me leave the room while they pick the number). I then pointed to each chart one at a time and I asked the class to tell me if the number they picked was on the chart. Then I told the students that they should all concentrate very hard on the number that the volunteer had picked and that they shouldn't try to trick me by thinking of another number. Then, after a few seconds of deep concentration, I told the class the number. As always happens, the students were very impressed by my mental powers, and they demanded I do the trick again.

After I had done the trick a number of times I told the students that I would show them what was going through my mind when they told me which charts their number was on. I mentally put the number one under every chart that contained their number and I put zero under every chart that didn't contain their number. For instance, the number thirteen is on charts A, C and D, so if their number was thirteen, I would have this picture in my head:

Chart D	Chart C	Chart B	Chart A
8 9 10 11	4 5 6 7	2 3 6 7	1 3 5 7
12 13 14 15	12 13 14 15	10 11 14 15	9 11 13 15
1	1	0	1

The ones and zeroes under the charts are just the binary code for the number thirteen. Similarly, the number nine is on charts D and A.

Chart D	Chart C	Chart B	Chart A
8 9 10 11 12 13 14 15	4 5 6 7 12 13 14 15	2 3 6 7 10 11 14 15	1 3 5 7 9 11 13 15
1	0	0	1

But 1001 is just the binary code for nine. I told the students that when they tell me which charts their number is on they are giving me the binary code for the number (many students figure this out for themselves with some hints). So I can always figure out which number the students pick by translating the binary code into a regular number. Once the students understood this they wanted to come up to the front of the class to do the trick themselves.

If I have enough time with a class, I always make sure that every student can do the trick. I invite weaker students up to the front of the class so they can show off in front of their peers. I then have the students pair off and practise with each other. In London, though, I ran out of time before I could teach everyone the trick.

On my second day at the school, I gave the students a lesson on adding and subtracting fractions that was rather mundane compared to the lesson on binary codes. Although the students were mostly in Grade 4 and working well below their grade level, I didn't feed them pizza or ask them to cut out pie diagrams or play with blocks to learn about fractions. I made them work individually at their desks with pencil and paper, and near the end of the lesson, to liven things up a little, I gave them longer and longer sums with larger and larger numbers.

On the third day, when Rachel and I stepped into the class for our lesson, the children cheered. They weren't accustomed to receiving such challenging work in mathematics, or such lavish praise for their accomplishments. They were clearly thrilled to be exercising their minds so vigorously and to be showing off to adults who expected so much of them. At the end of our last lesson the students crowded around Rachel and me to give us hugs and ask when we would be coming back.

When Rachel set up my visit to the school, she had arranged for Nikki Aduba, the manager of primary strategy for the school board, to meet me and observe one of my lessons. During our first meeting Nikki had a great many questions about JUMP and seemed skeptical about some aspects of the program. But her actions showed her qualities as a leader. She took the time to find out about the program and kept pressing me until she had gotten the answers she wanted. I could tell that Nikki was devoted to the students in her board from the way she behaved in the class she observed. The moment the lesson started, she jumped right in and started helping the kids.

Nikki and I continued our conversations by phone after I returned to Canada, and she came to Toronto for two days to observe the program at Queen Victoria Elementary School. When Nikki returned to England she ran a two-month

JUMP pilot with forty teachers and teacher's aides in twenty-four schools. The students selected for the pilot were all in Grade 5 but were achieving well below grade level. During the pilot the teachers used the JUMP fractions unit as well as material on number sense and numeracy from the JUMP workbooks. A report on the results of the pilot is posted on the JUMP website; it contains the following summary:

> The response to the JUMP pilot has been overwhelmingly positive, from the interest shown at the time that schools were first invited to participate, to the enthusiasm of the final review meeting. Without exception, all participating teachers want further involvement with JUMP, and continuing professional development in the philosophy and principles of the program, as well as access to the full range of JUMP materials and resources.

After the success of the summer pilot, the board ordered workbooks for five thousand students for the 2006–07 academic year. According to the board's report, the students in the summer pilot had made impressive academic gains on standardized tests and had also shown striking improvements in other areas:

> All teachers reported a significant improvement in attitude in the vast majority of pupils participating in the pilot. The children became far more confident and were eager to speak out and actively participate

during mathematics lessons. Teachers also commented on increases in self-esteem of pupils who had hitherto (for years in some cases) seen themselves as failures in the subject. Behaviour also improved; children who had been disruptive during the lessons were engaged, focused and enthusiastic during the JUMP sessions.

Teachers were particularly struck by the way the JUMP lessons held their students' attention; the students' level of enjoyment and engagement was something the teachers hadn't seen before in a math class. The report contains over thirty quotes from teachers remarking on how much the students enjoyed and benefited from the lessons. Here is a sampling:

There are no specific individuals who surprised me but the degree of success with ALL pupils, and the sheer joy math's suddenly brought to the children was a surprise.

The children are eager, cooperative and want to learn. If a child tries to be disruptive, another child is likely to reprimand. This is in direct contrast to when the sessions started.

From being easily defeated mathematicians who rely heavily on adult support, these children are now ballsy independent learners, full of confidence, desperate to show their skills, and lovers of maths!

The group selected for JUMP were suffering from a lack of confidence in most subjects, especially in maths. The buzz we created with JUMP meant that most of the class would approach me and demand, "Are we doing JUMP today?" and would be disappointed if we were not.

In the 1990s, while he was working with patients with obsessive-compulsive disorders, the neurologist Jeffrey Schwartz made a discovery that I believe has enormous implications for education. By using meditation to monitor their thoughts and focus their attention away from negative behaviours and towards positive ones, Schwartz's patients were able to produce permanent changes to their neural pathways. Schwartz and a number of other pioneers of neural plasticity, such as Michael Merzenich and William Jenkins, have discovered that "the simple act of paying attention produces real and powerful physical changes in the brain." According to Schwartz,

> Our brains allocate space to body parts that are used in activities we perform most often—the thumb of a video game addict, the index finger of a Braille reader. But although experience molds the brain, it molds only an attending brain. Passive, unattended, or little attended exercises are of limited value for driving neuroplasticity . . . 'Plastic changes in brain representations are generated only when behaviors are specifically attended.' . . . And therein lies the key. Physical

changes in the brain depend for their creation on a mental state of the mind—the state called attention. Paying attention matters. It matters not only for the size of the brain's representation of this or that part of the body's surface, of this or that muscle. It matters for the dynamic structure of the very circuits of the brain and for the brain's ability to remake itself.

I am convinced that the dramatic changes I have observed in weaker students are connected to the work I have done to help those students focus their attention. I have taught a number of students who initially couldn't seem to retain the simplest facts, or couldn't sit still for more than a few minutes at a time, or couldn't concentrate long enough to make the most elementary inferences. That these students were able to learn mathematics was only partially due to the strategies I developed for teaching the subject. I am convinced that deep psychological factors played as great a role in their progress as the mathematical content of my lessons. But these psychological factors are all but ignored in our debates about curriculum.

I am certain that attention can be trained. Just as there are exercises to help a limb paralyzed by stroke move on its own, there are exercises that will help a chronically distracted brain learn to focus. From my work in some of the most challenging classrooms in the school system, I am also convinced that it is far easier to train the attention of young children than one would expect. The studies cited by Schwartz suggest that without attention the brain does not remake or rewire itself. Without attention students cannot learn or retain information. And schools are generally not very good at capturing the attention of students who struggle or fall behind. The teachers in London were genuinely surprised that their students could be so engaged and attentive in math lessons, because this was not something they had seen before.

I believe we will never fully capture the attention of children until we stop conceiving of them as miniature versions of ourselves who have inherited all the likes and dislikes that we acquired from our own experiences at school. Our failure to understand what naturally excites children and motivates them to learn is evident in the textbooks and methods that some educational theorists have encouraged schools to use. The fact that so many students are struggling at school clearly shows that adults have gotten a great many things wrong about what engages the attention of children.

RELEVANCE

When I first met Kevin he was crouched on top of a desk in the middle of his classroom. None of the other students in his class, busy working at the desks around him, seemed to be concerned that he was getting ready to spring into the air and might easily land on someone's head. I said, "Hello, Kevin," and he growled at me.

After four or five lessons with a JUMP tutor, Kevin was able to sit on a chair for at least part of a lesson instead of lying or crouching on his desk or squirming around on the floor at his tutor's feet. Kevin's only real interests in life appeared to be professional wresting and bullying other kids. He couldn't read, even though he was in Grade 4. He spent most of his time in class distracting the other children. Sometimes Kevin's tutor had to be satisfied if he reached a hand up from under his desk to write something down.

Kevin's teacher told me that math paved the way for Kevin to become engaged at school. He had never had much success, because he couldn't read or focus on his work. Thanks to the efforts of his teacher he is now making very good progress in math and has even started to read. His behaviour and ability to focus have changed dramatically. Kevin always has a gift for me now when I visit him. If he knows I am coming, he will give me a drawing or sometimes a toy. But even when I surprise him he will present me with a well-used eraser or the stub of a pencil as if it were a real treasure. His pride in the work he has completed makes my visit worthwhile.

I have observed the kind of changes I saw in Kevin in at least fifty other students who were identified by their schools as having serious attention deficits or problems with behaviour. I have worked for a year or more in several classes for children with severe behavioural problems. In one class the teacher couldn't dismiss the kids until about twenty minutes after the bell rang at the end of the day, because every time they tried to form a line at the door they would start to push and shove each other, and would end up shouting and fighting and rolling on the floor. This may have been a regular occurrence, but the children always did their work during the math lessons. They were excited about doing advanced work and showing off their skills, just as the students in

London had been excited. And their behaviour outside the math class quickly started to improve as well, just as the behaviour of the children in the London pilot improved.

I regularly teach math lessons in elementary schools across Canada. Usually I can walk into a classroom that I have never visited, even in a difficult school, and generate some excitement about mathematics in the class. If I am able to work with a class for several days and get to know which students need extra help and which could benefit from extra challenges or praise, I can usually build a fair amount of momentum into the lessons. In classes where I have worked for extended periods, children often ask for extra work or to stay during recess. In one inner-city class that I visited for a year, the children demanded twenty pages of work for the summer and wouldn't let me go until I had assigned twenty pages to all of them. I have been at year-end assemblies where the entire school stood and cheered for the JUMP tutors and me, as though we were minor rock stars.

Of course, not all of my lessons elicit these kinds of reactions, and I sometimes give classes where I am sure I have bored some of the children or left others behind. But, for the most part, children seem to enjoy learning mathematics when I teach. I am not a naturally gifted teacher—I have met many who are more charismatic, funnier or faster on their feet, or who understand students better than I do. The excitement that students sometimes display during my lessons has always been a surprise to me, and to anyone who knows me. I am too old to be cool, and I am not, as I have said, a particularly dynamic or charismatic speaker.

I am, of course, very passionate about teaching math and about seeing students succeed. I used to think that it was the excitement I radiate when I teach that gets kids engaged in my lessons, but recently I had the opportunity to watch myself on video. During the lesson I had thought I was virtually jumping up and down with excitement, but the person in the video appeared to have taken Valium.

There is an element of novelty in my lessons that partly accounts for their success. I am a new face in the classroom and I don't have to deal with the endless problems that exhaust teachers and sometimes make them lose patience with their students. But the element of novelty cannot entirely account for the results I have seen, as many other teachers have produced exactly the same results in their own classes. The teachers in London, for instance, whom I met only after the pilot was finished, were of all ages and personality types and undoubtedly used a variety of styles in their lessons. But many of those teachers reported the same levels of engagement and improvements in behaviour that I have seen.

The last thing you would expect of kids who have struggled at school is that they would want to sit for long periods doing math, or that they would cheer for math, or that, as the teachers in London reported, they would be disappointed when math class was cancelled. These are kids who are normally demoralized and destroyed by math and who often end up dropping out of school because they find it so difficult. So why do kids get so excited about JUMP lessons?

There are some elements of the JUMP approach that obviously contribute to its success and that have little to do with the JUMP materials. We ask teachers using our materials to be very positive, to give lots of praise during their lessons and to create an atmosphere in class where students won't feel judged, especially if they make a mistake. I tell students that when I was their age I sometimes thought I was dumb and couldn't do math. I assure them that I won't think they are stupid if they make mistakes, because I sometimes make mistakes myself, and if they pay attention they might catch one of my mistakes. I also tell them, as I have mentioned, that if they don't understand something in one of my lessons, it's my fault for not explaining it well and they can stop me and ask me to explain it again. In JUMP implementation, fidelity to this philosophy and also to the methods of the program seems to play a greater role in its success than the personal characteristics and style of the teacher.

But I am convinced that it is not only the teacher's attitude that accounts for the way the JUMP lessons capture the attention of the students. I believe there is also something in the mathematical content of the lessons that they respond to. The JUMP fractions unit, which was initially created as a confidence-builder, appears to be the most foolproof of all the units I have designed. Oddly, it is also the unit that is the most abstract. I have received more than a hundred testimonials from teachers saying how excited their students became when they taught the unit. At first glance the fractions worksheets don't contain anything that children could ever get excited about. The material doesn't condescend to kids in any way, nor does it try to make fractions relevant; in the course of the unit students do very abstract and rather advanced symbolic manipulations with fractions, and nothing more. Many teachers have trouble believing that kids would find this kind of work interesting, until they have seen it in their own classes. (Fractions are taught in a more traditional way in the JUMP workbooks, with a mixture of concrete and symbolic work. The fractions unit is as much a unit on pattern recognition as it is on fractions.)

As adults we often project the negative experiences we had at school onto children. Fractions were the bane of many people's existence, as was mathematics in general. I have given a number of talks to students at teachers' colleges and have found that many pre-service teachers are extremely anxious about math. An instructor in one of the classes I spoke to told me she had asked her students to write a reflection about their experiences learning math in public school, and many had used the image of a jail or a torture chamber in their essays. A survey of students at university once revealed that students who planned to become elementary school teachers had the highest levels of anxiety about math of all the students. Teachers who are anxious about math or who dislike math sometimes find it hard to teach the fractions unit properly, because they don't believe their students could ever get excited about doing mathematical operations, particularly with fractions. Rather than getting excited about their students' success, they adopt an almost apologetic tone for putting them through such torture.

It is not uncommon for adults to be wrong about what children like. Some of the more dramatic examples of adults misunderstanding children have happened on television.

When the producers of *Sesame Street* first conceived of the show, they consulted education and psychology experts about what children might like to see on television, and early test episodes of the show were based on the insights of the experts. But when the producers observed children watching the show, they found that the experts were wrong about many of the features that eventually made it a success. For instance, the experts had warned that children would not be able to deal with a mixture of fantasy and reality. But when the producers monitored what children were paying attention to on the screen, they found they were most engaged when the Muppets interacted with the human characters.

The producers of the show *Blue's Clues,* which was created after *Sesame Street,* went even further in observing children to find out what they liked. Before the program aired, no one had thought that children would want to watch the same episode of a TV show over and over. But the producers of *Blue's Clues* decided to run each episode five times a week. By the end of the week, children who took part in the test screenings began to shout out answers to the characters' questions in advance—they loved knowing what was coming next. Anyone who has read a story to a child knows how much children love hearing the same thing over and over. In *The First Idea,* a book on how intelligence evolved in humans, Stanley Greenspan and Stuart Shanker present a great deal of evidence that suggests that infants develop cognitive abilities by learning to decipher subtle patterns in the voices, facial expressions and emotions of their caregivers. Even older children love to observe and create subtle variations on a pattern endlessly. According to Greenspan and Shanker these kinds of activities, especially when performed together with a loving and responsive caregiver or instructor, help develop and consolidate neural pathways in the child's brain.

In the fractions unit, similar-looking questions are repeated throughout the unit, with subtle variations that students love to spot. As the students work through the unit, they start to notice and anticipate the central patterns and variations, just as children do when they watch *Blue's Clues*. This kind of experience may seem boring to an adult, but the JUMP pilots have demonstrated that it is not at all boring to kids.

I once taught a Grade 5 class how to multiply numbers in which all the digits of the numbers except for the leading ones are zero. To multiply 2,000 x 30,000, you just multiply the leading digits (2 x 3 = 6), then count the total number of zeroes in both numbers and add that many zeroes to the result (since there are seven zeroes in the two numbers, 2,000 x 30,000 = 60,000,000). At the end of the lesson a boy came running up to show me his work. Using the technique I had just taught the class, he had multiplied two twenty-digit numbers. There was barely enough room on the page for his work, so his answer was wrapped around the margins. To an adult, what he did might seem an extremely boring and trivial exercise. But judging from the boy's excitement, he seemed to believe he had demonstrated that my procedure worked all the way to infinity—and he was also undoubtedly proud to show me that he could work with such enormous numbers.

We will never fully develop the potential of children until we recognize that they are unimaginably different from adults. Adults think that repetition is tedious, so they fail to give children the practice they need to consolidate their understanding of skills and concepts. Adults think that familiar facts are boring, so they seldom ever give children enough time to explore those facts. Adults think that extending an obvious pattern is pointless, so they don't allow children to test that a pattern goes on forever, nor do they allow them to demonstrate their amazing ability to handle more and more complex variations on a simple theme. Adults rarely raise the bar for children very effectively or capture their attention in mathematics, because they don't know how to see the world through the eyes of children. I have seen many classes jump up and down with excitement simply because I made the numbers in a question larger, and because I gave the weakest students a chance to show off. Whenever I give a lesson that I'm not happy with, it is usually because I have underestimated how naive children are and how much they enjoy repeating things and taking blindingly obvious steps. (Of course a teacher should also not underestimate how sophisticated in their thinking children can be.)

Practice doesn't have to be painful for children, and repetition doesn't have to involve what teachers call "drill and kill." If teachers are careful to introduce subtle variations into the work they assign, if they constantly raise the bar without raising it too far and if they make learning into a game of different levels and twists and turns, then kids will practise and train effortlessly.

Children in Canada are now required to work from math textbooks in which a great many new terms and concepts are introduced on each page, and the pages are crammed with pictures and information. While these books contain some very good exercises and explanations, all the extra bells and whistles as well as the amount of new information introduced on each page, can actually distract or confuse children. A study that appeared several years ago in *Scientific American* found that the more complex a pop-up book is, the less effective it is for teaching reading. The authors of the study speculate that this is probably true of materials for older children as well. In Asia, where students do much better in math, the texts are extremely spare.

When designing the JUMP workbooks, JUMP staff and I deliberately made the layout very simple. We also tried to reduce the number of words on each page and to introduce only one or two new concepts per page. There is a great deal of consistency in the design and in the way the topics are introduced at each grade level, with similar formatting in many of the questions, so that the material seems familiar to children who have been in the program for some time. Teachers in the London pilot thought their students might not like our workbooks because they didn't have a lot of pictures or flashy designs, but they reported afterwards that the children loved them.

People who design math textbooks and programs for children are usually experts in the curriculum but not in the psychology of children. Textbooks are rarely given the extensive testing that TV shows such as *Sesame Street* and *Blue's Clues* undergo. Even if the theories underlying the pedagogy of the books happen to be correct (and there is some question about that, as I will discuss in chapter nine), there is still a huge gap between theory and its implementation in a text or program. I have written dozens of worksheets that I thought were perfect until I tested them in classrooms and realized that there was too much information on the page, or that I had failed to provide enough preparation or practice for the students, or that there were conceptual barriers hidden in the material that I hadn't noticed. Considering how different children are from adults, educators would be wise to test whether the texts and programs they produce actually engage the attention of children. Our failure to pay attention to what they find interesting is evident from the number of students who are completely disengaged from school by Grade 6. If the school system were a TV show, it would be off the air by now.

There is a push now in math education to make everything relevant to children. Unfortunately, from the perspective of adults this means making everything cool or based on examples from real life. One problem with this approach is that most adults don't really know what is cool or relevant to kids. In a Grade 7 text, I came across a long story about a band called the Geometrics that students have to read before they can answer some questions on geometry. In one of the questions, students are asked to design a CD cover for the band, but they must follow some rather implausible specifications. Apparently the band's record company has decided that the CD must have a trapezoid, a triangle and a parallelogram on the cover, and they have even specified the percentage of the cover the figures can occupy.

Apart from producing material that is sometimes cool or interesting only in the eyes of adults, the attempt to provide a context for everything in math forces kids to wade through a great deal of text before they actually get to a math problem. Frequently kids who are weak readers or who speak English as a second language fall behind unnecessarily because of the language in the textbooks. Some educators seem to assume that kids will never find a mathematical problem interesting unless it comes dressed in a story. From the way I have seen kids react to wordy textbooks, I would say that they find abstract operations with fractions more relevant and engaging than a far-fetched story about a rock band.

It is certainly a good idea to teach mathematics using examples from real life. But there was a time when textbook writers were able to get to the point of a word problem concisely and elegantly. Kids can certainly benefit from reading longer stories that involve math, but only if the stories are well written and if the language does not become a barrier to the mathematics. Books by science fiction and fantasy writers can spark the imaginations of children by making them see how magical the universe is, but the characters in mathematics textbooks today often seem to be limited to making geometric logos for T-shirts or playing with blocks.

By insisting that children must be taught according to their developmental level and that *everything* they learn must be framed in a rather mundane, "relevant" context, educators risk removing any sense of enchantment from learning. Children would undoubtedly find mathematics and science more interesting if they were introduced to the deepest and most beautiful ideas in those subjects at an early age. Countless fascinating topics in pure and applied science require only elementary math that we don't have to wait until high school or university to teach. JUMP is now developing a series of books, Enriched Lessons in Mathematics for Every Student. Some of the titles in this series will be *Mathematics and Magic Tricks, Mathematics and Nature, Mathematics and the Environment, Mathematics and Sports, Mathematics and Art, Mathematics and Secret Codes* and *Mathematics and Music*.

To spark children's imaginations I have given several different lessons on theoretical computer science to students from as early as Grade 3. The students were able to complete the tasks I gave them and they often asked me to extend the lessons. I start one of my lessons on computer science by showing students how to draw a theoretical model of a computer called a finite-state automaton. Students then try to figure out what kind of patterns their computer will recognize by moving a penny around on their sketch like a counter in a board game. Following a suggestion from my daughter, I once gave kids in a Grade 3 class paper clips to hold their drawings in place on a cardboard folder. Rather than using a penny as a counter, the kids put a pair of fridge magnets on their drawing, one on the front and one on the back, and they used the back magnet to pull the front one around like a cursor. The children even drew little keyboards for their computers. Many of the children mentioned this lesson in their thank-you letters to JUMP; even though they had only a partial understanding of finite-state automata, in their minds they had made real computers.

Math consultants for a school board in Eastern Canada once observed a JUMP lesson on how computers read binary codes, which was similar to the lesson I gave in London that I described at the beginning of this chapter. After the lesson the teacher was barred from using JUMP in her class because the lesson hadn't been taught developmentally. And I recently received a very negative review for the same lesson from a math consultant working for an education ministry.

We need a much broader definition of relevance in education. Games that have no connection to the world, such as checkers, are relevant and interesting to kids, and so are games that use mathematical symbols, even if those games don't have direct applications to the child's life. As long as the games have clear rules and ways of winning, and as long as the students have enough success, they will find the games interesting and meaningful.

This is what we have missed completely in our obsession with making math relevant to kids. It is the structure of the experience as much as the actual content of the lesson that is interesting to kids. Success is relevant. Momentum is relevant, and so is the possibility of advancing to higher levels in a task (that's why children love video games). Being able to show off in front of your peers is relevant. And, finally, understanding or accomplishing something collectively, with your entire class, is relevant. Sometimes trying too hard to make math relevant—in the narrow sense of the word, by giving everything a context—can actually get in the way of things such as success or the momentum of a lesson that are also relevant to children.

CONFIDENCE

I have never met an educator who would agree that students who lack confidence in their intellectual abilities are likely to do well at school. I find it surprising, therefore, that no program of mathematics used in our public schools has ever taken proper account of the role of confidence in learning. If students are more apt to do well in a subject when they believe that they are capable of doing well, it seems obvious that any math program that aims to harness the potential of every student must start with an exercise that will build the confidence of every student.

Many teachers have used the JUMP fractions unit to build the confidence of their weaker students and to get their entire class engaged in learning mathematics before moving into the regular curriculum. While the unit has proven very effective, I certainly don't think that a confidence-building unit necessarily has to involve fractions, nor does it have to look anything like our unit. But while I don't think a confidence-building unit needs to look like the fractions unit, I believe that any unit that seeks to engage weaker students without boring faster students will probably have to have certain features in common with the fractions unit. I will sketch out some of the criteria that I think a confidence-building unit will likely have to meet.

1. An exercise that aims to build the confidence of weaker students must only require that students possess a very small set of skills to complete their work successfully. It must be possible to teach these skills even to the most

challenged students in a short time. And a teacher must be able to verify easily that every student in their class has acquired the necessary skills before they start the exercise. In a typical public school, even in Grade 3, an enormous gap in knowledge, ability and motivation exists between the weakest and strongest students. Any exercise that aims to build the confidence of weaker students must take this gap into account. The exercise should not demand too much of weaker students, or the purpose of the exercise will be defeated right from the start. In the fractions unit students are only required to add and subtract one-digit numbers, and to multiply and divide by the numbers two, three and five. Weaker students are taught to do these operations on their fingers in a very efficient way. (Many students complete the unit not needing to use their fingers anymore.)

2. In classrooms where mathematics has been taught in a traditional way, students usually work at very different speeds. To keep students who are initially faster from getting bored, an exercise that seeks to build the confidence of weaker students must provide (or show teachers how to design) extra work for students who finish early. In the fractions unit, there are two or three sections of worksheets for almost every topic. In the first section (the A section), students who can do the simple operations mentioned above can answer all of the questions. The B and C sections contain harder-looking questions with more steps that require operations with slightly larger numbers. But all of the questions in the B and C sections are on exactly

the same topic as those in the A section. Hence faster students can move ahead into these sections with little or no extra help, and the teacher can spend more time with weaker students. As soon as all the students finish the A section, the teacher moves on. All of the questions on the final test for the unit involve questions of the sort that appear in the A section, so all of the students can do well on the test.

I have always been surprised at how excited students will become at answering bonus questions, even when those questions are only incrementally harder than the regular work. Children love showing off to a caring adult: if teachers are excited when they assign the bonus questions then faster students will be excited about solving them. And this excitement will spill over to the slower students as well. In every class where I have taught the fractions unit, the slower students have always started racing through their worksheets so that they could be assigned bonus questions too. (And often kids who were initially slower started outpacing kids who were initially faster.)

I always make up special bonus questions for the most challenged students too, so they can feel that they are doing harder work as well. For instance, when a weaker student can add the triple fractions with the same denominator, I will say "Do you think you can handle four fractions?" and write a question like 1/17 + 1/17 + 1/17 + 1/17 across the bottom of their page. Students respond enthusiastically to this kind of challenge. Many teachers have remarked on how surprised they are at how weaker students can keep up with faster students when they are confident and are given the skills they need to keep up with the lessons.

3. An exercise that seeks to build the confidence of weaker students must recognize that for many children (especially in inner-city schools) language can be a barrier to mathematics. As a mathematician, I believe that students should be taught to explain and discuss mathematical ideas. But based on my experience teaching hundreds of children, I also believe that exercises that demand a substantial amount of reading and writing should be introduced into the elementary mathematical curriculum very carefully and incrementally. Before children can read and write fluently, they must acquire an enormous number of visual, motor, auditory and cognitive skills.

In mathematics, on the other hand, even concepts used by working mathematicians can be reduced to one of two extremely basic operations, namely the operation of counting or the operation of grouping objects into sets. (Logicians proved this over a hundred years ago.) The vast majority of children are able to perform these operations at an early age, so mathematics is a subject they can excel at long before they become expert readers. If we were to remove language skills as a barrier to learning math, I am certain that their sense of confidence and ability to focus, as well as the conceptual abilities children would develop in that subject, would have an effect in other subjects.

To elaborate, this is not to say that children should not be taught to explain their work or communicate about mathematical ideas: in the grade-specific JUMP workbooks, these skills are taught incrementally in a very rigorous and effective way. Many teachers who have used the fractions unit have reported significant improvements in their students' ability to concentrate and to focus on printed materials, as well as in their ability to see patterns, to perceive what changes and what stays the same in a sequence of symbols, to follow chains of inference and to generalize and extend rules to new cases. These are exactly the skills that a child must possess in order to become a fluent reader.

In our public education system, we now try to teach reading and literacy at the expense of mathematics by loading too much language into our elementary textbooks. By neglecting to ever teach elementary students math in a purer form, as a symbolic language in its own right, we neglect a tool that could help students become more literate. If we were to use less language in the early part of our math programs (and introduce it more carefully in the later part) and if we were to allow students to sometimes play math more as a game of manipulating symbols, generalizing rules and seeing patterns, I predict that we could accelerate students' development as readers.

I recommend that teachers think of the fractions unit—in part—as an exercise in reading (or a preparation for reading) for weaker students. Rather than having to grapple with the twenty-six letters of the alphabet and a vast number of ill-defined rules for combining those letters, students can experience mastery in a more simple symbolic universe that contains only a handful of symbols (i.e. the numerals from zero to nine as well as a few operation signs) and a handful of rules for combining those symbols. A teacher should not underestimate the degree of effect that working with the material necessary for working out fractions—manipulating these mathematical symbols mentally and copying and lining the symbols up properly on the page—will have on the development of a student's ability for reading and writing.

4. Whenever new concepts or new rules or operations are introduced, the teacher must be able to quickly verify that every student has understood the new material. And the teacher must find it easy to provide extra help quickly and efficiently for students who need it. Textbooks and programs of mathematics are rarely designed to take account of the difficulties teachers face in large classes. Current philosophies of education advocate that children be encouraged to explore and discover mathematical ideas in somewhat open-ended problem solving lessons. While I agree with this approach as one of the goals in math education, I also believe that it is a mistake to start a math program with too many lessons of this kind. Children who struggle with math, or who have trouble focusing, are often left behind.

If a teacher's aim is to engage all of their students—not just the ones who are more advanced than their peers—and if children must be confident and attentive to learn, then it seems obvious that the teacher must start their math program by assigning work that every student can complete without the help of their peers. When students work in groups, or when the teacher doesn't have a means of constantly checking what the weakest students know, those students can easily lose focus. The unit must be designed to allow teachers to identify and help students who need remediation immediately, so that all students gain the confidence they need to do more independent work.

5. An exercise that aims to build the confidence of weaker students must allow the teacher to raise the bar incrementally so students can experience the thrill of meeting a series of graduated mathematical challenges. In my experience, children who are having difficulty in their schoolwork respond much more quickly to praise and success than to criticism and threats. Of course, a teacher must be firm with students and must establish clear rules and boundaries, but I've found it's generally easier to get kids to adhere to rules and to respect others if they feel admired and successful.

I have worked with a great many children with attention deficits and behavioural problems over the past fifteen years and I have had a great deal of success simply by raising the bar. If I encounter a student who I think might cause problems in a class, I'll say: "You're very smart. I'd better give you something more challenging." Then I give the student a question that is only incrementally harder—or that only looks harder—than the one they are working on. (I rarely give a challenge to a student who is having difficulties unless I'm certain they can do the question.) I always make sure, when the student succeeds in meeting my challenge, that they know I am impressed. Sometimes

I even pretend to faint (students always laugh at this) or I will say: "You got that question but you'll never get the next one." Their excitement accelerates when they succeed in meeting a series of graduated challenges. Of course a teacher doesn't have to use my exact methods: teachers find different ways to encourage their students, but I think passion is essential.

6. An exercise that aims to build the confidence of weaker students should expose them to a body of knowledge that has a degree of unity (so students can see how skills and concepts they learned for one topic apply to another) and that is rich enough to allow students the experience of ascending through the levels of a rather substantial structure (like climbing a mountain and looking back at the series of cliffs you've scaled). It also helps if the material in the exercise is perceived by students to be difficult and advanced.

Fractions underlie all of mathematics and are generally thought to be impossible for some students to master. Many students first start to struggle in math when they are introduced to fractions. When elementary students see that they can do the work that older kids often struggle with, they become convinced that they are good at math. In the fractions unit, one skill builds on another, so that students always have to think carefully about which method they should use for answering a question. For instance, after learning to add fractions by changing both denominators, students are taught to check if one denominator divides into the other in case they can add the fractions more efficiently. They then learn to extend this skill to add mixed and triple fractions.

Many math programs for weaker students consist of endless drills in basic skills. Because children who struggle in math are generally assumed to be incapable of doing more advanced work, they gradually lose all confidence and motivation so that, even after several years of extra help in math, they can scarcely remember the simplest facts. Many of the children who enter the JUMP program have not, after five or six years of regular school, managed to learn even the three-times table. I have come to believe that one of the best ways to motivate children who have fallen behind is to skip them ahead—to convince them that they are capable of doing work beyond their grade level. The remarkable progress weaker students have made in the fractions unit shows the enormous role a student's perception plays in learning. Clearly, students learn more quickly if they feel they are doing advanced work and succeeding.

I first started teaching fractions to remedial students because I thought that it might motivate them to learn their times tables. A fact learned while practicing challenging mathematics is more readily recalled than one learned by rote drill: when students constantly have to multiply and divide in the course of adding and reducing fractions, they become extremely motivated to learn their times tables. Often students who were not previously inspired to do extra work will ask to learn higher times tables so they can work on the B and C sections.

GROUP WORK

Marilyn Burns has said, "Sitting still and doing independent work limits opportunities for learning." There is certainly some truth to this idea; a program that was based only on individual work would not allow kids to learn things by communicating with other kids. But lately I have begun to wonder whether schools are relying too much on group work. I am not certain about this, but I will present some of my reasons for thinking so.

Over the past ten years I have worked with a great many children who had developed significant attention problems by Grade 3 or 4. In some schools I have seen kids wandering the halls during class and kids who couldn't sit still for more than a minute without having to jump up or yell out or pinch or poke someone. In some schools there is a consistently high level of noise and a steady stream of disruptions. But in classrooms where children are allowed to experience individual success and where they have been given the means to become deeply engaged in independent work, students become more focused and their hyperactivity and disruptive behaviours tend to disappear. This observation has been confirmed by many teachers who used JUMP methods and materials. In the Grade 3 pilot I described in chapter two, the children who had been identified as having attention deficits were able to sit still for thirty minutes and write a very challenging exam. Having seen such dramatic changes in behaviour in classrooms that have implemented JUMP, I have recently begun to wonder if the high incidence of attention deficits I have observed is being exacerbated by the classroom environment.

When I was reading Schwartz's book *The Mind and the Brain,* the results of one experiment caught my eye. Using food as a reward, researchers at the University of California in San Francisco trained seven adult owl monkeys to

> discriminate among vibrational frequencies applied by a mechanical device to a single spot on one finger. The flutter vibration felt like the flapping of a bird wing. The frequency, but not the location, of the stimulus varied . . . Six of the seven trained monkeys got better at recognizing when the frequency changed. At first they could detect a change only when frequencies differed from a 20-hertz (twenty flutters a second) standard by at least 6 to 8 hertz. But over the course of training the monkeys learned to discriminate differences as small as 2 or 3 hertz.

The researchers found dramatic differences in the brains of the monkeys after they were trained: the parts of the brain that controlled the stimulated hands showed significantly more cortical activity than the parts that controlled the non-stimulated hands. To test whether it was the vibration itself that caused the changes or the monkey's attention to the vibration, the researchers applied the same flutter vibration to the fingers of a new group of monkeys, but used a repeated tone to distract the animals. The distracted animals had no meaningful brain changes. If the monkeys' attention was focused elsewhere while they received the same tactile stimulation that had produced massive cortical remapping in the other monkeys, no such reorganization occurred.

While it may seem quite a leap from training owl monkeys in a laboratory to teaching children in a classroom, I believe the experiments are connected to something I have observed in my students. For a skill to become automatic or for knowledge to really sink in, the student must be able to focus on the task at hand without too much distraction. Most of my work with children involves finding ways to achieve and maintain a heightened state of attention. It seems likely to me that consistent distraction can prevent the human brain from registering the effects of repeated stimulation or training. The research with the monkeys and other experiments Schwartz cites, many of them involving humans, show a definite difference between what happens in the attentive brain versus the distracted brain.

In classrooms engaged in group work or activities, the distracting single tone of the laboratory can sometimes be multiplied many times, and the various distractions can affect almost every sense. There are loud noises, constant movements, the giving and the taking of materials, the pushing and pulling of fellow students, debates about who has more or less or who didn't get the colour they wanted or who should sit where. These constant distractions likely make it harder for children to learn things that require a great deal of practice and attention. And children who don't have the opportunity to learn or practise basic skills at home suffer the most.

One purpose of group work is to teach children to cooperate, but in our extensive reliance on group work we may again be mistaking the ends (that children learn to work together) with the means for producing those results. Children may actually learn to work productively in groups more quickly if they are first taught to work independently and if their self-esteem, motivation and attention have been nurtured through success in individual work. In many inner-city schools children are expected to work together before they have developed the social skills, self-esteem or sense of focus that they need to benefit from that work.

A PhD student once told me she had videotaped Grade 8 kids doing group work over an extended period of time. When the students were interviewed about the work they had done, they said they had worked cooperatively during the lessons and confirmed that they had done all the things the teacher had asked them to do to solve problems together. But when the PhD student watched the video, it brought her to tears: she observed a great deal of subtle bullying and ostracism during the lessons. When she re-interviewed the kids they admitted that they had indeed bullied and ostracized some of the students, and that they made those statements about being cooperative only for the sake of the teacher.

There are teachers I respect who swear by group work, so I believe that lessons based on group work can benefit students. But from what I have observed in many classrooms, I also believe that a teacher must have a great deal of skill and knowledge to make group activities work for all the students.

This is particularly true in inner-city schools, where there are vast differences between weaker and stronger students. I am certain that many students are not adequately prepared to do group work and that they are being unnecessarily left behind by always being compelled to learn in groups. Schools need to test methods of instruction that are based on group activities more rigorously to find out when they work (for all children), what effect they have on attention, at what age they should be introduced, and what proportion of student work should be done in groups.

One reason group work has become so prevalent is that we have confused sitting still and doing independent work with being passive. But, as I pointed out earlier, being motionless is not the same as being passive. One of the greatest gifts teachers can give their students is to teach them to travel by sitting still, with no other baggage than a pencil and paper and no other vehicle than their imaginations. The fallacy in education is that there are only two alternatives—either students sit alone passively or they work actively in small groups. But there is another alternative that combines the benefits of group work and individual work, and I will present this way of working in chapter seven. But before we can understand its benefits, we need to examine some educational myths more closely.

—

CHAPTER FIVE

THE TRIBE THAT COULDN'T COUNT

—

HERE'S AN EXPERIMENT you can try at home, provided you have the right equipment. You will need ten ordinary kitchen glasses and a five- or six-year-old child. Place the glasses on a table in two rows, with five glasses in each row. The rows should be parallel and the glasses in each row spaced equally apart. Ask the child (the subject) if there is the same number of glasses in each row. If all goes well, the subject will say yes. Then rearrange the glasses in one of the rows so they are farther apart, making the row appear longer. Keeping a neutral expression on your face (so that your experiment will meet the highest standards of scientific rigour), ask the subject again if there is the same number of glasses in the rows. Don't be alarmed if the subject answers incorrectly. In one of his most famous experiments with children, the psychologist Jean Piaget found that many of his subjects gave the wrong answer, even when he rearranged the glasses right under their noses. Piaget thus concluded that five- and six-year-old children lack a reliable sense of conservation of number.

Two decades after Piaget conducted his groundbreaking experiments, researchers began to wonder if he had correctly interpreted the responses of his subjects. When three- and four-year-olds were asked the same question that stumped the older children, they saw right away that when a row of objects is stretched out it still contains the same number of objects. If Piaget's claims were correct, then five- and six-year-old children mysteriously lose an ability they possessed when they were two years younger. Researchers proposed the following answer to the puzzle: at age five or six children begin to understand other people's motivations. Confronted with exactly the same question in two different situations, Piaget's subjects likely assumed that the person asking the question expected a different answer each time. This interpretation of Piaget's results was supported by another experiment, in which a teddy-bear puppet rearranged the objects while the experimenter's back was turned. Five- and six-year-olds had no trouble seeing that the two rows of objects contained the same number of things, even after the naughty teddy bear had popped up and wreaked havoc on one of the rows.

In another well-known experiment, Piaget discovered that an infant playing with a toy will not try to find the toy when someone hides it under a blanket. He concluded that the infant must believe that the object no longer exists. More recent research has suggested that infants fail to look for hidden objects because they lack the motor skills required to retrieve them, not because they think the objects have dematerialized.

Piaget's experiments led him to postulate that children pass through a series of developmental stages that limit their ability to reason and develop higher-level conceptual abilities. In Piaget's view, children generally move from a concrete stage, in which they understand the world almost exclusively through physical models, to an abstract stage, when they can begin to understand formal or symbolic operations and abstract thought. His theories were fundamental in the creation of current educational programs, which are based on the idea that children should not be introduced to operations and algorithms (an algorithm is a procedure for doing something in math, such as the steps in long division or for adding fractions) until they have spent a great deal of time playing with concrete materials and manipulatives.

Some educators believe Piaget's theories imply that children must be taught almost exclusively with concrete materials until they advance past the concrete stage. According to such educators there is no point in teaching children concepts before they are at the appropriate developmental stage, because they will neither understand nor retain the concept and may even be harmed by being introduced to the concept too early. Following this logic, if a student fails to progress when taught by this method, the student is not capable of entering the abstract phase and will never be able to perform or understand symbolic operations. This view has had a profound influence on our public school system in the past two decades. Mathematical concepts are introduced in our schools by using concrete materials such as pattern blocks, base-ten blocks, Cuisenaire rods and hexagonal and circular pies, and children are not encouraged to perform complex operations with mathematical symbols until they have spent years playing with the things those symbols represent.

Piaget was a brilliant psychologist and he broke new ground in his field, but the conclusions he drew from some of his experiments show how easy it is to draw incorrect inferences from children's behaviour and how difficult it is to build general theories about their cognitive development. I believe that current educational theories about how children develop mathematical concepts, particularly the theory that children must always move from the concrete to the abstract, are simplistic and prevent us from nurturing the true mathematical potential of children.

Many schools have adopted textbooks and mathematics programs that seem to assume that, given enough time and a little guidance from a teacher, children who play with concrete materials will naturally develop an understanding of numbers. But even the simplest concrete materials do not provide transparent representations of mathematical concepts. I have seen children in a remedial class reduced to tears when their teacher tried to show them how to regroup (or borrow, as it used to be called) using base-ten blocks, and I have encountered enormous numbers of children in inner-city schools (sometimes half of a class) who cannot add or subtract proficiently, even though they spent the first four years of school doing daily exercises with a great variety of manipulatives.

To use concrete materials effectively, it helps to understand their limitations. These teaching aids do not, unfortunately, wear their interpretations on their surfaces. Recently in the jungles of the Amazon, scientists stumbled upon a tribe whose members have been catching and sharing large quantities of fish since prehistoric times, but who can't say exactly how many fish they've caught when there are more than two in the net. The Pirahã tribe has words for only *one, two* and *many,* and they appear to be incapable of counting or matching small collections of objects, even with coaching. This example shows quite clearly that mathematical concepts don't necessarily spring into people's minds when you slap a concrete object (a fish, for instance) into their hands.

Some scientists believe that the Pirahã are incapable of understanding mathematics because of the constraints imposed on their thinking by their language. According to Peter Gordon, a scientist who has studied the tribe, "the lack of number words seems to preclude the ability to entertain number concepts. There may be other ways to learn and represent exact numbers but in the normal course of human learning language is the route we take." In cognitive psychology a good deal of evidence suggests that it is not only the words we use to name physical objects and quantities, but also the formal and grammatical structures of our language that help determine our perception of the physical world. Alexandre Borovik, in "Coxeter Theory: The Cognitive Aspects," explains:

When infants learn to speak (in English) and count, there is a distinctive period, lasting five to six months, in their development, when they know the words one, two, three, four, but can correctly apply only the numeral "one," when talking about a single object; they apply the words "two, three, four," apparently at random, to any collection of more than one object. . . . the children at this stage [are called] one-knowers. The most natural explanation is that they react to the formal grammatical structure of the adults' speech: one doll, but two dollS, three dollS. At the next stage of development, they suddenly start using the numerals two, three, four, five correctly. Chinese and Japanese children become one-knowers a few months later—because the grammar of their languages has no specific markers for singular or plural in nouns, verbs, and adjectives.

When the native language is Russian, the "one-knower" stage is replaced by "one-(two-three-four) knower" stage, where children differentiate between three categories of quantities: single object sets, the sets of two, three or four objects (without further differentiation between, say, two or three objects), and sets with five or more objects.

Children who speak Russian learn to distinguish different categories of objects at an earlier age than English-speaking children because the differentiation of plural forms in the Russian language goes further than in English.

one doll	одна кукл**а**
two dolls	две кукл**ы**
three dolls	три кукл**ы**
four dolls	четыре кукл**ы**
five dolls	пять кук**ол**
•	•
•	•
•	•
ten dolls	десять кук**ол**

While it might appear that children learn the names of quantities simply by associating number words with collections of objects, their grammatical understanding of number can precede their use of words that name concrete things. "[A]n infant's brain is tuned exactly at picking the rules: it is easier for the child to associate the number of objects with the morphological marker in the noun signifying the object than with the word *one* or *two*."

When I first learned that the grammatical structure of a language could play a role in a child's perception of number, it brought many of my observations of students into focus. Mathematics itself is a language with its own grammatical rules for creating sentences, even if those sentences are often made up entirely of abstract signs that stand for things such as variables and operations. In calling mathematics a language I am not referring simply to the words that we use to talk about mathematical concepts. Mathematical symbols, such as the numerals (0, 1, 2, 3, . . .) or the signs that represent various operations (for instance, +, -, x, ÷,√, d/dx), as well as the rules that allow us to combine and generate strings of symbols, are all part of the language of mathematics. And so are the many icons and visual short forms we use to represent the physical world, such as the Cartesian plane, or the grid that I used to teach Matthew how to slide shapes.

To many mathematicians the symbols of mathematics and the rules that govern the manipulation of those symbols often seem to have a life and substance of their own that are richer and deeper than the physical models on which mathematics is based. Mathematicians are often led further into the realm of abstract ideas by the very structure of the language they use, just as infants are led into the realm of numbers by the structure of their native tongue. I maintain that an understanding of the structure of math as a language can help lead children towards an understanding of the concrete.

Mathematics was invented for practical purposes: for counting sheep and measuring fields. In the modern world, through its applications in science and industry, mathematics is the source of virtually all our material comforts. But mathematics became effective as a material tool primarily by becoming an abstract language in its own right. Over the centuries mathematicians have made discoveries more often by seeking to understand the logic or internal structure of that language than by following their intuitions about the physical world. The nineteenth-century mathematicians who discovered the laws of curved space did not intend to launch a revolution in the physical sciences, as happened when Einstein applied their ideas in the twentieth century. They simply wanted to make the axioms of geometry a little more concise. Richard Feynman, Nobel laureate and one of the great physicists of the past century, once said, "I find it quite amazing that it is possible to predict what will happen by mathematics, which is simply following rules which really have nothing to do with the original thing."

Einstein's famous equation $E = mc^2$ is clearly an abstract or symbolic representation of a physical law. But the floor plan of a house is also a symbolic representation: a set of lines drawn on flat paper that bears little resemblance to the three-dimensional house it represents. Similarly, the calculation a carpenter makes to determine how many nails are needed to build the house is entirely different from the act of counting out the nails. Mathematics, even in its most practical applications, in carpentry or finance or computer science, is a game of inventing and manipulating symbols. And mathematical symbols and the operations by which they are combined are very different from the things they represent.

To understand this point it helps to consider the operation of adding fractions. This operation is based on two rules:

1. If the denominators of a pair of fractions are the same, you add the fractions by adding the numerators (keeping the denominator the same).

2. To make the denominators of a pair of fractions the same, you may multiply or divide the denominator of either

fraction by any number as long as you do the same thing to the numerator.

These two rules have various physical representations: you can show children how the rules work by cutting pieces of pie or by lining up fraction strips. But you can also teach children to add fractions without ever showing them a physical model of a fraction.

Of course, I don't advocate that children be taught mathematics without concrete materials; the JUMP workbooks are filled with exercises that show students how mathematical rules are embodied in physical models. But it is important to notice that the rules listed above don't make any mention of pies or blocks or fraction strips. Everything you need to know to perform the operation of adding fractions is given in those rules. And they are simple enough that virtually any eight-year-old can learn to apply them flawlessly in a matter of weeks (as has been demonstrated conclusively in dozens of JUMP pilots). By focusing exclusively on representative models we have lost sight of how utterly easy it is for children to learn the individual steps of an operation (such as the addition of fractions) when those steps are isolated and taught one at a time.

I believe that a child's understanding of mathematics as a language or symbolic game can play as great a role in the conceptual development of that child as his or her concrete experience of the world. And I believe this perspective is sorely needed in elementary classrooms. For the purposes of education we should view concepts as embodied equally in the concrete models and in the language we use to communicate in mathematics. This language includes the words, the symbols, the rules and procedures—in essence, the grammatical structure of mathematics—that people use to do mathematics. The concepts do not lie exclusively in one domain or the other. When we insist that elementary concepts are embodied only or primarily in concrete models, we limit a teacher's ability to instruct efficiently and to reach all students.

I was led to appreciate the importance of symbols and language in a child's understanding of mathematics through my work with the most challenged students in JUMP. I had seen the effect of the fractions unit, in which children play at math as a symbolic game, on children who were struggling with the subject. Noting the striking improvements in children who had done the unit, I began to wonder whether children's understanding of the structure of mathematics as a language might sometimes precede their concrete understanding of mathematics. The idea that teaching children to understand math as a language might sometimes accelerate their understanding of the concrete, rather than the other way around, was really brought home by my work with Matthew.

Even though Matthew was in Grade 4 when we started our lessons, he seemed to have no perception of numbers. If I put two pennies on the table and then put down three more pennies, he couldn't tell me there were five pennies on the table without counting them. Often he would have trouble even counting the pennies consistently, losing track of which ones he had or hadn't counted. If I showed him any pair of numbers greater than five he couldn't tell me which number was larger. No matter how often I tried to get Matthew to add or subtract by using pennies and other concrete materials, nothing seemed to work; he couldn't match or count small sets of objects with any degree of proficiency. Like the members of the Pirahã tribe, he seemed to be incapable of seeing numbers.

One day I recalled that Matthew knew the names of all the characters in the Harry Potter books, including the Weasley twins. So I wrote the following numbers on a piece of paper:

1 4

2 3

I told Matthew that the pairs of numbers that add up to five are like twins and, like the Weasley twins, he could think of them as being from the same family. I said I would call them "magic twins" or "magic pairs," because once he knew the names of the twins he could start to add and subtract.

I found a deck of cards and removed all the cards greater than five, so that only the cards from ace to four remained. I dealt four cards to Matthew and four to myself. I told Matthew that if he had any magic pairs in his hand he could put them on the table. Then he could ask me for any card that would make a pair with one of his cards. For example, if he had an ace he could ask me for its twin—the four, and if he had a two he could ask me for a three and so on. If I had the card he asked for I would have to give it to him and he could then put the pair down on the table. If I didn't have the twin he wanted, I would say, "Go fish," and he would have to pick up the top card of the deck. Then it would be my turn. The winner would be whoever put down all his cards first. (Later I made the game more interesting by giving one point for each pair put down and three points for whoever went out first.)

We played a few hands, and Matthew laughed hysterically whenever he beat me. He clearly enjoyed playing the game, but I couldn't figure out why, even though I had given him the chart to help him remember the magic pairs, he couldn't play unless I checked his hand to give him hints. After playing several hands I realized that I had violated one of the first principles of JUMP: before you assign a task or problem, always verify that your student has the skills or conceptual knowledge necessary to complete the task. I had neglected to teach Matthew to sort his cards, so he found it impossible to see the magic pairs even when he had only four cards in his hand.

To teach Matthew to sort his cards, I placed three cards that included a magic pair on the table in front of him and asked him to find the pair. After some practice he was able to find the pair immediately. I then slowly increased the number of cards that I put down and the number of pairs I included in the set. I made a game of the exercise by challenging Matthew to find the pairs as quickly as he could. I pretended to be mad at him whenever he was able to beat my rather generous time limit, and he found this very funny. Soon he was able to sort his cards without any assistance from me.

As soon as Matthew knew the pairs of numbers that add up to five, I changed the game so that he had to remember the pairs that add up to ten. At first he couldn't remember all of the pairs, so I made a chart that showed the various combinations: 1 and 9, 2 and 8, 3 and 7, 4 and 6 and 5 and 5. I gradually covered up the pairs until he knew them all by heart. To help Matthew remember them, I occasionally played a modified game of Monopoly with him. I drew pictures of Monopoly houses on cards and wrote down their prices, which were all between one and nine dollars. I held up a card and told Matthew to imagine that he had just paid me ten dollars for the house, and then I asked him to tell me how much change he was supposed to get back. If the house card had "$8" written on it, Matthew would tell me that I owed him two dollars.

I have played the Monopoly house game with a number of students, and it worked particularly well with an autistic girl. She was extremely anxious about math and her anxiety seemed to interfere with her ability to remember number facts. To help her calm down when we were playing the game, I pretended I was a real estate agent and that I was trying to get her to buy a house. I made up a story for each house—for instance, "This house costs only two dollars. It's a real dump. It has a bathroom, but it's in the garden"—and I told her she could tell me how much change she was supposed to get back whenever she was ready. One day she cut me off in the middle of my sales pitch and told me the correct change. I must have looked surprised because she started to laugh at me. This routine became part of our game: I would start my story and she would cut me off and laugh when I looked surprised or pretended to be angry with her. She could take as much time as she wanted to tell me how much change I owed her, so she didn't feel any pressure to remember the magic pairs, but there was always a payoff when she did remember a pair. The game helped her learn the pairs very quickly. I always try to improvise when I am teaching, and I constantly watch my students to see what they respond to—I believe this is the main reason I have had success with weaker students.

Matthew's ability to recall and do operations with the magic pairs began to deepen when I taught him the algebraic relations between the pairs. I made a number of worksheets of various equations relating the pairs, with empty boxes where Matthew could fill in the missing number of a pair. The relations for the pair two and eight are

$$8 + \_ = 10 \quad \_ + 8 = 10 \quad 2 + \_ = 10 \quad \_ + 2 = 10$$

$$10 - \_ = 8 \quad 10 - 8 = \_ \quad 10 - \_ = 2 \quad 10 - 2 = \_ \quad 8 + 2 = \_$$

After a little practice Matthew could fill in the missing number in any equivalence that involved the pairs. Then he could also do calculations that involved multiples of ten. If I asked him what 100 - 80 was, he knew the twin of eight was two, so he could me tell the answer was twenty. That meant he could calculate the change he would get from a dollar if he paid eighty cents. He could also do more sophisticated calculations. To find the difference 100 - 36 he would reason as follows: the twin of six is four, so I can add four to thirty-six to get to the nearest multiple of ten (i.e., forty). But one hundred take away forty is sixty. So 100 - 36 is sixty plus the four, or 100 - 36 = 64. I also showed Matthew the patterns that occur among the magic pairs when you write them in a column.

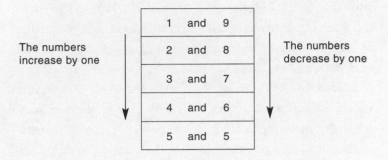

In spite of Matthew's growing proficiency at recalling and manipulating symbols, he still did not have any real sense of numbers. He knew the names of the magic pairs, and their relations, but he had no idea what those things meant in terms of physical objects such as blocks and pennies. I wasn't sure if the work we had done would have any effect on the way he perceived sets of objects. So, when I was certain that Matthew knew the algebraic relations between the magic pairs automatically, both for five and for ten, I placed five pennies in a row and showed him how to make models of all the relations he had learned.

I pulled one penny away from the end of the row and said, "Look, five take away one leaves four," and then I put the penny back in the row and said, "And one plus four makes five." I made Matthew show me all the ways he could pull apart and put together combinations of five, then ten, pennies, and I insisted that he tell me out loud which relation he was making a model of in each case. After about fifteen minutes of this exercise I said, "Matthew, what do you think the magic pairs for the number seven are?" and he immediately replied, "One and six, two and five and three and four." I put seven pennies on the table and Matthew was able to show me all the relations that he saw. I was surprised that the work we had done with the five and ten had transferred so quickly to other numbers. Before we started our exercises, Matthew had not even been able to see numbers, let alone make predictions about them. He is now increasingly able to use numbers in daily life to solve problems.

A number of factors might explain why the approach I took with Matthew worked, and it is important to try to separate these factors. The most obvious reason for its success is psychological: I made learning into a game. I did everything I could to ease Matthew's fear of mathematics by breaking things into steps and raising the bar incrementally. Because Matthew was not anxious, and because he was always led forward by the expectation of new success and new challenges, he was able to focus his attention and learn much more quickly. The second reason had to do with memory: I had chunked various representations of the things I wanted Matthew to learn. Memory works better when facts are connected in a web of knowledge. Matthew could use various ways of thinking about the symbols for the pairs and their models—he could associate them with a card game, with

Monopoly cards, with the algebraic games we played and with the manipulations he had done with pennies. The more parts of the brain a child has to call on and the more associations he can make, the easier it is to recall a concept.

But I believe there is a deeper reason why Matthew was able to develop a concrete sense of numbers out of the symbolic work we did. Some children see the world differently from the average person, and not necessarily because they are less intelligent. In some ways children like Matthew are a great deal smarter than the average person. But because they see the world differently, they can appear to be incapable of grasping certain kinds of concepts.

Matthew sees the world in extremely vivid detail. He can, for instance, glance at twenty pictures of trains and tell you which one he rode in Vancouver last summer. Once, when his mother was teaching him about parallel lines, she drew the following figure:

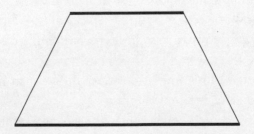

She asked Matthew if the horizontal lines (in bold) were parallel, and he said no. She was surprised by his answer because he had been able to identify all the pairs of parallel lines in his JUMP workbook. She asked him why he thought the lines in the figure weren't parallel and he replied, "Because they're not the same length." When his mother and I discussed this problem we realized that in the examples we had used to teach Matthew about parallel lines, and in the questions in the workbook, the parallel lines were all the same length. So Matthew had inferred that lines are parallel if they run in the same direction and they are the same length. Because he is so hyper-perceptive he had noticed something in the workbooks that I hadn't seen myself. In the next edition I made sure to include some examples of parallel lines that were not the same length.

The South American writer Jorge Luis Borges once wrote a story about a man who sees the world in such detail that he has trouble understanding how people associate particular names with physical things. If someone were to point to two robins and say, "Those are two robins," the character wouldn't be able to see why anyone would want to give the two birds the same name. Because he sees every feather and every streak of colour in so much detail, the birds would seem to him to have very little in common. I suspect that Matthew sees the world in much the same way: parallel lines that are the same length look very different to him from ones that are a different length.

But how could knowing the names of and symbolic relations between the magic pairs have helped Matthew see relations among concrete materials? Because of all the work we had done, he knew how to represent the pairs symbolically in various ways—in words, in numerical and algebraic expressions and in images (the playing cards and

Monopoly cards). He knew that the pairs always went together, no matter which type of representation he might be thinking about or where the representation was stored in his brain. The name "two" went with the name "eight"; a playing card with the number two on it went with a playing card with the number eight, no matter what suit the cards were in; the empty spaces in the algebraic expressions

$$8 + \_\_ = 10 \quad \_\_ + 8 = 10 \quad 10 - \_\_ = 8 \quad 10 - 8 = \_\_$$

could be filled with the number two. Matthew knew, therefore, in many different contexts, that the magic pairs always formed a kind of binary opposition: if one appeared, he knew he should look for the other, just as infants know subconsciously, from the grammar of their language, what to look for in small groups of objects. I believe this symbolic knowledge helped Matthew see which sets of pennies formed the magic pairs. He also knew that the pairs could be arranged in a pattern: if you increase a number in a magic pair by one, then by decreasing the other number in the pair by one, you create a new magic pair. Knowing this allowed Matthew to predict the magic pairs for the number seven.

The confusion that Matthew once experienced when he tried to connect concrete quantities to abstract rules is simply an extreme form of the confusion that many children experience when they try to learn mathematics. Doing symbolic work can help a child perceive (and also be more motivated to perceive) the concrete world more clearly, just as an unconscious awareness of the grammatical structures of a language can make a difference to the age at which a child can perceive certain sets of numbers. As a species we have evolved to use symbols to help us organize and clarify our ideas and our perceptions: our facility with the formal and symbolic structure of a language clearly helps us understand the world.

In my opinion there are other reasons for teaching kids at an earlier age to learn math as a symbolic game. For one thing, it is extremely easy to teach the rules and operations of mathematics—one of the easiest things to teach even the most challenged students—so kids can get a psychological boost from doing symbolic work that can make them more motivated to do math. I have seen evidence of this with the JUMP fractions unit. Second, there is a great deal of conceptual work implicit in symbolic work that I believe has been overlooked by some educators, and this work must be done before kids can truly understand math. Learning to understand math symbolically is as conceptual as learning to understand it concretely.

Let's suppose that there are some benefits to teaching children math as a symbolic game while, or sometimes even before, they are learning to understand mathematics concretely. Some educators think you can actually harm children by teaching them symbolic rules and operations in math at an early age. If this is true, then the drawbacks of teaching rules and operations at an early age must outweigh the benefits. Why do educators think this?

There is a general feeling in education now that formal or symbolic work is mechanical, and that if teachers place too much emphasis on mathematical or grammatical rules they will turn children into uncreative robots. But this view doesn't take into account the way writers and mathematicians develop new ideas. When a poet finds the right word to fit a particular rhyme scheme, he also finds a connection between images or ideas that he hadn't previously seen. The exercise of fitting thoughts into a form—of polishing a sentence to make it more elegant or symmetrical, of searching for a word that will echo or play against another word—can lead a writer to entirely new thoughts. And when a mathematician tries to make a set of rules or axioms more elegant entirely for beauty's sake, she discovers new things about the world. The mathematician Hermann Weyl once spoke of the "uncanny effectiveness of mathematics," referring to the fact that solutions of purely formal problems in mathematics often have profoundly important applications. But Weyl might just as well have spoken of the uncanny effectiveness of language. The formal structures of any language, whether they are grammatical, literary or symbolic, do not prevent original thought—they compel it.

It is extremely easy to teach any operation so that students learn the steps of the operation perfectly and also have a complete understanding of what the steps mean. To explain how this is possible, I will sketch a method of teaching the algorithm for long division. This approach helps students understand and perform the algorithm perfectly, but it also allows them to discover how the algorithm works by themselves. Many students find long division very hard and most never learn it properly, even by high school, so it's the ideal operation to illustrate how easy it is to teach algorithms.

Before students learn long division they must have some method of finding the answer to simple division questions such as 15 ÷ 5. I sometimes play the following confidence-building game with weaker students before I introduce the concept of division. I developed this game after a tutor told me that one of her students, a girl in Grade 4, had refused to let her teach her how to divide. The girl told her tutor that the concept of division was much too hard for her and she would never consent to learn it. I suggested that the tutor teach division as a kind of counting game. In their next lesson, without telling the girl she was about to learn how to divide, the tutor wrote the numbers fifteen and five one after the other. Then she asked the child to count on her fingers by multiples of the second number until she had reached the first.

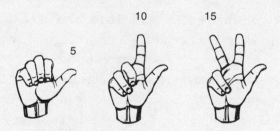

After the child had repeated this operation with several other pairs of numbers, the tutor asked her to write down, for each case, the number of fingers she had raised when she stopped counting. For instance,

15　5　<u>3</u>

As soon as the student could find the answer to any such question quickly, in each example the tutor wrote a division sign between the first and second number and an equal sign between the second and third.

$$15 \div 5 = 3$$

The student was surprised that she had learned to divide in ten minutes. When I teach weaker students to divide by this method, I often raise the bar by having them skip-count by fives to higher and higher numbers.

The division statement 15 ÷ 5 can be interpreted in two ways, so there are two ways in which the action of skip-counting by fives can be related to a model of division. In the first interpretation, the statement 15 ÷ 5 can be taken as asking how many sets of five can fifteen objects be divided into. Under this interpretation, students can practise making models of various division statements by using objects such as blocks, pennies or counters or by drawing sets of lines or dots. For the expression 15 ÷ 5, students draw or place groups of five objects successively until they have fifteen objects altogether. They end up with three groups, so fifteen divided into sets of five is three. As students make the groups I sometimes have them skip-count by fives, raising a finger each time they create a group, so they can see that the number of fingers raised corresponds to the number of sets they have made.

ONE WAY OF LOOKING AT DIVISION

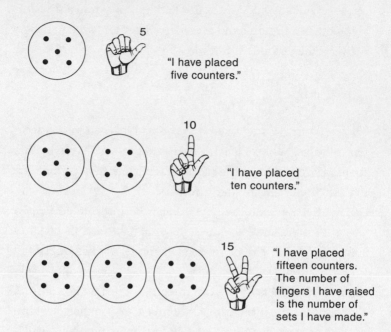

"I have placed five counters."

"I have placed ten counters."

"I have placed fifteen counters. The number of fingers I have raised is the number of sets I have made."

Under the second interpretation, the statement 15 ÷ 5 can be taken as asking how many objects would be in each set if fifteen objects were divided into five sets. Students can draw five circles to represent the five sets; they then place one object at a time in the circles until they have placed fifteen objects. As they place the objects I will often have students skip-count by fives, raising a finger each time they finish placing one more object in each of the sets (the number of fingers raised is the number of sets created).

A SECOND WAY OF LOOKING AT DIVISION

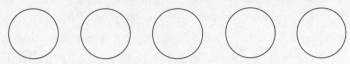

"I want to make five sets, so I draw five empty circles."

"I have placed one counter in each set, giving five counters altogether."

5

"I have placed another counter in each set. The number of fingers I have raised is equal to the number of times I have placed an object in each set."

10

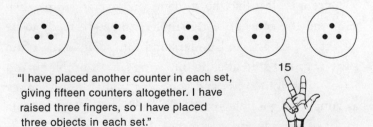

"I have placed another counter in each set, giving fifteen counters altogether. I have raised three fingers, so I have placed three objects in each set."

15

143

There are many other ways to look at division. It may be seen as repeated subtraction (you can subtract five from fifteen three times before you get zero, so fifteen divided by five is three); as skip-counting on a number line (it takes three skips of five to get to fifteen, so fifteen divided by five is three); as the inverse of multiplication (three times five is fifteen, so fifteen divided by five is three) and so on. In the JUMP workbooks all these ways of looking at division are introduced one at a time—along with a good deal of practice. Students are also taught to distinguish word problems in which the number of sets is being asked for from problems in which the number of objects in each set is being asked for.

Before I teach the long division algorithm, I also teach students to understand the concept of a remainder. To find $17 \div 5$, weaker students can use counters to model the problem, but they can also skip-count by fives until they get as close to seventeen as possible. When they are skip-counting, students will stop at the number fifteen with three fingers raised, so they know they can place fifteen objects in three sets of five. With seventeen objects originally and fifteen placed in the three sets, two objects are left over.

Once it is clear that the students understand simple division and the concept of remainders, they are ready to be taught to perform and understand long division. I often start by giving students the following sort of problem: You have eighty-four cents and you want to divide the money as equally as possible among three friends. I ask students to make a model or drawing of the problem with dimes and pennies, using as many dimes as possible. The model will look like this:

I tell the students that the standard way of writing a division statement such as 84 ÷ 3 is 3)84. I create a number of division statements and ask students to say for each statement how many sets the coins are to be divided into (that is, how many friends are there?) and how many dimes and pennies they would need to make a model of the problem.

3)84

number of friends? _3_
number of dimes? _8_
number of pennies? _4_

I don't move ahead until I have checked that all the students understand the meaning of the division statement. Once they do, I ask them to draw three circles to stand for the three friends in the question. Then I ask them to divide the eight dimes in their model into the three circles, or sets, as equally as possible. Students quickly see that they can place only two dimes in each of the sets and that they still have two dimes and four pennies left over.

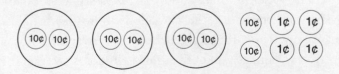

Students can see from their model that to find out how many dimes each friend receives they simply have to divide eight (the tens digit of eighty-four) by three (the number of sets being made). I give students a test on this one skill, giving them room to fill in only the number of dimes that each friend gets, before I move on.

$$3 \overline{)8\,4}^{\,2}$$

number of friends (or sets) 3

number of dimes (or tens) in each set 2

After the students have got perfect marks on my test, I ask them how they could calculate in any division question—without making a model—how many dimes are given to each friend. Students quickly see from their model for $3\overline{)84}$ that they multiply the number of sets (three) by the number of dimes placed in each set (two). I ask them to do this calculation and to write their answer under the tens digit in the division statement.

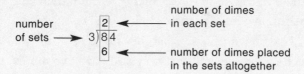

number of sets → number of dimes in each set

number of dimes placed in the sets altogether

When students understand the first two steps of long division perfectly, I ask them to tell me how they could calculate how many dimes are left over after each friend has received an equal share of the dimes. Students see that they simply have to subtract the number of dimes they placed in the sets from the total number of dimes in their model.

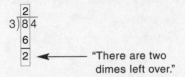

"There are two dimes left over."

I then give students a number of questions so they can practise at the first three steps of the algorithm.

To teach the next step in long division, I ask students to look at their model and divide the money represented by the two leftover dimes and the four pennies evenly among the friends. Students see that they first have to exchange the two dimes for twenty pennies before they can divide up the money. After exchanging the dimes, they have twenty-four pennies altogether.

Very few adults can explain why you bring down the number in the ones column in long division:

"I bring down the four because I have exchanged the two dimes for pennies—I now have twenty-four pennies."

But there is no great mystery here. You bring down the number four in the ones column because, to divide up the remaining money, you must exchange the two leftover dimes for twenty pennies, which you then combine with the four pennies that you originally had to make twenty-four pennies.

Now, to divide the twenty-four pennies among the friends you start the whole process over again. With a weaker class I teach each of the steps below separately and verify that students have understood the step before I move on. With a more advanced class I challenge the students to figure out the remaining steps themselves.

THE FINAL STEPS OF LONG DIVISION

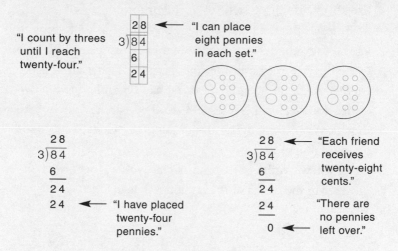

"I count by threes until I reach twenty-four."

$$3\overline{)84} \quad 2\,8$$

"I can place eight pennies in each set."

"I have placed twenty-four pennies."

"Each friend receives twenty-eight cents."

"There are no pennies left over."

After students have learned to explain the steps of the division algorithm using dimes and pennies, I often have them repeat the exercise using base-ten blocks.

The steps in the long division algorithm are themselves so trivial that even the weakest students can master them quickly, especially as they become more excited and more focused when they see how easy the steps are. And none of the steps in any mathematical operation are harder than the steps I have shown for division, so there is no reason why students can't learn any operation. Whenever I teach an operation I always have a stock of bonus questions on hand for faster students, in case the weaker students need more time to master a step. I find that a minute or two of extra practice is all the weaker students often need to keep up with the faster ones.

When I teach an operation to a class that is behind or that has trouble focusing, I sometimes teach the steps of an operation before I introduce the model for an operation in detail. I find it much easier to control a difficult class, and to capture their attention by constantly raising the bar, if the students work individually on worksheets or on questions I have written on the board. Success often makes the weaker or more disruptive students more motivated to eventually work with concrete materials and to understand why the operations work. This is particularly true of students who have given up on school or who are convinced they can't learn mathematics; I find I am able to keep their attention if I give them tasks they can have immediate success with, and if I make sure there is no opportunity for them to be diverted from the task by a partner or by searching for the right material to build a model. With difficult classes I often use diagrams to explain why a step works until the class is focused enough to work with concrete materials. Other teachers might find it easier to work with challenging students by using models first, but I find it helps to focus a class by starting with operations and diagrams.

But now to address the educators who believe that, if children learn the rules for an operation before they completely understand how to model its steps with concrete materials, they will never fully understand the operation. I agree that there is substance to this concern. In the past teachers often taught students how to perform the steps of an operation without ever explaining why the operation worked. That is why teachers should constantly check whether their students have a concrete understanding of the operations they are performing. Even in our fractions unit, which was designed to allow kids to play with symbols and patterns and to gain confidence in math—and not to teach fractions completely—we recommend that teachers illustrate with pictures (or models, if they prefer) why the operations work. Many students finish the unit with a full understanding of operations with fractions, even though that is not the intention of the unit. (Fractions are taught completely using models and diagrams in JUMP workbooks.)

Sometimes students who learn an operation without having first been taught the model for it habitually apply the operation without any real thought, and as a result they make mistakes that they are unable to spot. This is the chief danger in teaching an operation without first teaching the model. Faced with students who perform operations without understanding them, I show them the connection between the model and the operation and I frequently check that they understand what they are doing. I have always found it fairly easy to break the habit of performing operations without thinking by asking them to explain what they are doing and by giving them trick questions that require some thought.

I believe that generally teachers should introduce operations either by having students explore and develop them using models or by having them practise and explain the steps of an operation using both symbols and models at the same time (as in my approach to the long division algorithm). But I also believe there are times—particularly with students who have lost their confidence or who are disruptive or have trouble paying attention, and with large, diverse classes—when the benefits of teaching an operation symbolically before it is taught concretely outweigh the disadvantages of this approach. Which balance of concrete and symbolic work is most effective will likely depend on the level of the student and the style of the teacher. I believe that generally the safest method is to spiral back and forth between the concrete and the symbolic.

Many educators seem to have a naive faith in concrete materials. They believe that certain standard concrete materials, such as base-ten blocks and pattern blocks, will always work with a capable student: if students fail to learn with these materials, then there is not much a teacher can do for them. But, as I have pointed out, some students learn better if they are first taught symbolically or through a combination of symbolic and concrete work.

Teachers also need to be more creative in the way they use concrete materials and in the kinds of materials they work with. Many teachers teach students to subtract 7 - 5 by counting out seven objects, such as blocks or counters, and then taking away five of the objects. While it is important that kids learn this model of subtraction, it has serious drawbacks. You can't use this approach for larger numbers, as it would take forever to put out all the blocks, and challenged students could lose track of how many blocks they counted out. But there is a more serious drawback to this approach that is usually not taken into account in the debates about concrete materials: because the approach doesn't work for larger numbers, it is almost impossible to raise the bar effectively.

I often teach weaker students to subtract 7 - 5 as follows: they say "five" with their fist closed and then count up to seven, raising one finger at a time. The number of fingers raised when they say "seven" is the answer. This approach has a number of advantages. It gives them an embodied sense of how far apart numbers are. Students have an effective tool for performing subtractions quickly when the numbers aren't too far apart—a tool they can't lose and don't have to share or find or argue over with other students. Also the teacher can immediately start raising the bar with this approach. (Of course the teacher must ensure that the numbers being worked with—no matter how large—are within ten digits of each other.) I have made many Grade 5 classes start jumping up and down simply by writing a series of subtraction questions on the board with larger and larger numbers.

I believe that, with a balanced approach that combines symbolic and concrete work, kids could learn operations at a much younger age than they are taught in North America. I also believe that the idea that it is harmful to teach operations too early arose because in the past we did such a bad job of teaching operations and of showing students the connection between the operation and the model. A math consultant once told me that research in math education has proven that children should not be taught to do symbolic operations with fractions until Grade 7, and even then the operations should be taught primarily with concrete materials. When I heard this I was surprised, as I have taught many children much younger than twelve to completely understand operations with fractions, using diagrams and lots of practice with the algorithms, and occasionally some exercises with concrete materials. The consultant didn't seem to be aware that many Asian countries introduce children to operations with fractions in Grades 3 and 4. Children in those countries score higher in international math tests than children in Canada and the United States, where, ironically, the research on fractions originated.

When the consultant told me about the research I didn't think it was anything I needed to worry about, as I doubted that many parents or teachers believe kids can't learn to do operations with fractions until Grade 7. The research didn't correspond to anything I had observed in children, and I suspected that it was based on flawed experimental design or dubious theories about how children learn. But two years later I was shocked to see that the new Ontario curriculum mandated that children not be taught operations with fractions until Grade 7, and that teachers spend a great deal of time introducing them to the operations by using a variety of concrete materials.

The textbooks that are now used in Ontario all teach fractions in essentially the same way. When an operation is introduced, Grade 7 students have to explore it with at least four kinds of concrete materials, all of which can be purchased either from the textbook company or a company associated with the textbook company. The same textbooks are now in use across Canada, because the curriculum in every part of Canada is based on the American research that I mentioned. Ironically this research is now being called into question in the States, by mathematicians and a growing number of educators and cognitive scientists. (See Appendix 1).

Not long ago I came across a page in one of the textbooks that made me suspect that whoever wrote the material had either never taught in a classroom or was more interested in meeting ministry standards than in producing material that would help students. In the first question students are asked to add three pairs of fractions using pattern blocks (blocks in the shape of triangles, diamonds and hexagons that the school has to buy). In the second question they are asked to add four fractions using fraction strips. In the third question they have to add four fractions using number lines. (To add using fraction strips you have to divide the strips into smaller parts, using a ruler, so that the strips have the same number of parts; or, you have to purchase strips that have already been divided into parts. To add with number lines, you also have to divide the number line into the correct number of parts, something that requires already knowing the lowest common denominator of the fractions you are adding.) Several questions later students have to multiply four fractions by finding arrays and placing counters on the arrays.

Anyone who has ever stepped into a Grade 7 classroom, particularly in an inner-city school, can imagine how a class might go if the teacher tried to follow the textbook. The students would have to get out four different kinds of concrete materials to answer fifteen questions. Adding 1/2 + 1/3 with fraction strips, for example, would take an extremely long time, as the students would have to line up a half and a third strip, and then search among all of their strips for one that had the same length (the five-sixths strip). Apart from the question of what students would learn from doing so many exercises with concrete materials that they couldn't learn from a diagram (or a few examples presented by the teacher) and the amount of time it would take to find the right kind of fraction strip or the right set of arrays divided into exactly the right number of parts—for each question in the textbook, there is also the matter of classroom management. Grade 7 and 8 kids aren't the easiest to manage, and there would likely be a fair amount of confusion involved in finding and sharing the necessary materials. (And the concrete work could have been done at an earlier age: by Grade 7 students should be able to add fractions without constantly having to use models.)

We underestimate children by assuming that they will enjoy learning only concepts that have obvious physical models or applications. While I wouldn't discourage a teacher from serving pieces of pie or pizza to the class to illustrate a point about fractions, this is not the only way to get kids interested in math. Children will happily play a game with numbers or mathematical symbols, even if it has no obvious connection to the everyday world, as long as the game presents a series of interesting challenges and has clear rules and outcomes, and if the person playing the game has a good chance of winning. Children are born to solve puzzles; in my experience they are completely happy at school if they are allowed to exercise their minds and show off to a caring adult. What children hate most is failure. They generally find mathematical rules and operations boring only because those things are often poorly taught, without passion, in a manner that produces very few winners.

Children acquire new languages more readily than adults. Mathematics is itself a kind of language, with its own rules and grammatical structure. Why not let them become fluent in the language of mathematics when they are most ready to learn it? JUMP instructors have noticed that Grade 1 and 2 students often learn the fractions unit as quickly as—or more quickly than—children who are much older. Many fundamental mathematical concepts can neither be embodied in nor explained by a concrete model. As early as Grade 7, students encounter concepts and operations that have no physical explanation. Operations with negative numbers were first introduced in mathematics as a means for solving equations, and for centuries mathematicians multiplied negative numbers without knowing how to make sense of the operation. Leonard Euler, the greatest mathematician of the 1700s, even said that negative multiplication shouldn't be allowed, because it was senseless.

It's easy to see why a negative number times a positive number is a negative number. Consider, for instance, $-3 \times 2 = -6$: if you have a debt of three dollars and you double your debt, you end up with a debt of six dollars. But why should a negative times a negative equal a positive? A math consultant once told me she explains negative multiplication as follows: "When you multiply negative two by negative three, you subtract a debt of two three times, which gives a gain of positive six." But a clever student might say, "You taught me that multiplication is a short form for repeated addition. Why now, when both factors are negative, does multiplication suddenly become a short form for repeated subtraction?" Telling students to think about negative multiplication as repeated subtraction or as the rotation of a number line, as some consultants advocate, are not bad ways of helping them remember the rule, but unfortunately these approaches do not explain the rule. No physical model we can point to explains why the meaning of multiplication changes from repeated addition to repeated subtraction (or guarantees that this way of thinking about multiplication is consistent with the rest of mathematics).

If the rule "a negative times a negative is a positive" has no physical explanation, why should we accept it as a rule of mathematics? And how has a rule that is not determined by any aspect of the physical world proven so useful in physics and in other sciences? Mathematicians found the answer to the first question only in the 1800s; the answer to the second question remains a mystery. To understand why a negative times a negative is a positive, it helps to look at the rules, or axioms, of mathematics that govern the addition and multiplication of positive numbers.

If you add the numbers three and five and then multiply the sum by two, the result is sixteen. But you get exactly the same result if you multiply three by two and five by two and then add the products:

$$(3 + 5) \times 2 = 3 \times 2 + 5 \times 2$$

Sums and products of positive numbers always satisfy this simple equivalence, which is called the law of distribution. In the 1800s mathematicians realized that if the law of distribution is to hold for negative numbers, then a negative times a negative must be defined as a positive. Otherwise the law produces nonsense: if you define a negative times a negative as a negative, you can easily prove, using the distributive law, that the sum of any two negative numbers is zero.

This is an example of what I mean when I say that mathematicians are led more often by the internal logic of mathematics than by physical intuition. Because negative numbers had proven to be so useful for solving problems, mathematicians decided to extend the distributive law (which holds for positive numbers) to negative numbers. But then they were forced to define negative multiplication in a particular way. The rule for negative multiplication has found countless applications in the physical world, even though there is no physical reason why it should work! This is one of the great mysteries of mathematics: how do rules that have no straightforward connection to the world (and that are arrived at by following the internal logic of mathematics) end up having such unreasonable effectiveness?

I always thought that I was a bit of an idiot in high school for not understanding negative multiplication (and, even worse, multiplication of complex or imaginary numbers). My teachers often implied that the rules for these operations had models or explanations, but I was never able to understand the explanations. If my teachers had told me that math is a powerful symbolic language in its own right, and that the world of our everyday experience is described by a tiny fragment of that language (as I later learned in university), I believe I would have found math somewhat easier and much more interesting. The results of JUMP have shown that young children have no fear of the symbolic side of mathematics; they are much more open-minded and more fascinated by patterns and puzzles then most adults. If children were taught to excel at the symbolic game of math at an earlier age, they wouldn't encounter the problems that most students face in high school.

—

CHAPTER SIX

ANTHILLS AND HOLOGRAMS

—

WITTGENSTEIN TRIED TO SHOW philosophers the way out of the fly bottle of philosophy by getting them to pay closer attention to the meanings of words. Just try to define a simple word like "game." Wittgenstein pointed out that if you say a game has to involve luck or have a winner or be fun, you will always be able to find an example of a game that doesn't fit your definition. When philosophers give words overly precise or restrictive definitions, when they ignore the complexity and the irredeemable vagueness of language, they often fall into confusion.

Debates over the meanings of abstract words seldom have any effect outside of philosophy, but when words have religious, political or economic meanings, the debates can often turn into wars. The educational wars that are now being fought around the world over subjects such as reading and mathematics usually revolve around the meaning of one particular word. One day neurologists may discover precisely what the word "concept" means. But if that day ever comes it will likely be far in the future. At present, as a first step towards resolving unnecessary wars, educators must recognize that *concept* is as imprecise and complex in its applications as the simple *game*.

If you cut a hologram of a rose in half, the two parts will contain a great deal of information about the original picture, even if the parts look entirely different. And the information in the hologram is contained at every scale, so the smallest part of the picture allows us to reconstruct the entire rose. Concepts are also, in a sense, holographic. The same concept can be embodied in representations that look entirely different (for instance, in abstract symbols and in physical objects) and it can be embodied at different scales—in small steps and in big ideas—all at the same time. If you dissect a concept into its symbolic and concrete parts or its bigger and smaller parts, each part will reflect or contain information about the others. When Matthew learned to see the patterns in the symbols and algebraic equations for pairs of numbers that add up to ten, it helped him perceive and make predictions about how physical objects are combined in addition. Similarly, when I teach my students to add numbers on their fingers and they discover that it is easier to count up from the greater number—regardless of whether that number is to the right or the left of the addition sign—in this apparently trivial step forward they have begun to grasp the importance of the big idea that addition commutes.

As I explained in chapter two, it is often impossible to see any meaningful behaviour in the individual actions in an anthill. Groups of ants swarm around the entrance of a nest with no apparent pattern or purpose until the right number of patrol ants arrives at the right frequency and the colony begins to forage for food. In students conceptual understanding often emerges in the same way. Out of a number of repetitive activities or small steps that may not in themselves seem to be conceptual, and that may sometimes even seem disorganized, fragmentary and purposeless, deep understanding can emerge.

The hologram and the ant colony are only rough metaphors for concepts; they create pictures that capture something of the quality of concepts, but they do not define or fully characterize them. In this chapter I look at a number of pictures that have influenced the way teachers and educators think about terms such as *concept* and *conceptual understanding*. And I will argue that these pictures have held us back from nurturing the potential of children, because they are either inaccurate or incomplete.

The picture of elementary mathematics that many educators now have is very simple. Children engage in two extremely different types of mathematical activities: activities that involve understanding and conceptual thought, such as inventing a new method of calculation or solving a problem by making a model with concrete materials, and activities that are mindless and involve rote application of rules, such as solving a problem by doing long division or adding a pair of fractions by finding a lowest common denominator. This way of looking at mathematics is very similar to the way educators used to look at reading. Until recently many schools adopted a "whole language" approach to reading: educators assumed that comprehension and a love of reading would emerge naturally in children who were allowed time to immerse themselves in books. According to this view, teachers didn't need to emphasize basic skills or the mechanics of reading by teaching phonics or decoding skills. Mathematician and educator Huang Wu has written an excellent article on this issue titled "Basic Skills Versus Conceptual Understanding: A Bogus Dichotomy in Mathematics Education." According to Wu,

> Education seems to be plagued by false dichotomies. Until recently, when research and common sense gained the upper hand, the debate over how to teach beginning reading was characterized by many as "phonics vs. meaning." It turns out that, rather than a dichotomy, there is an inseparable connection between decoding—what one might call the skills part of reading—and comprehension. Fluent decoding, which for most children is best ensured by the direct and systematic teaching of phonics and lots of practice reading, is an indispensable condition of comprehension.

The idea that conceptual understanding in mathematics does not depend on—and is even opposed to—the teaching of basic skills, algorithms and procedures has shaped the curricula of school boards across North America. Many educators have called for minimizing the teaching of facts, rules and procedures in mathematics. In an influential article titled "The Harmful Effects of Algorithms in Grades 1–4," Constance Kamii and Ann Dominick claim, "Algorithms not only are not helpful in learning arithmetic, but also hinder children's development of numerical reasoning . . . Children in the primary grades should be able to invent their own arithmetic without the instruction they are now receiving from textbooks and workbooks."

The NCTM standards released in the nineties recommended that teachers put less emphasis on memorization of facts, the symbolic side of math, and any work that involves algorithms and procedures, including "complex paper-and-pencil computations," "paper-and-pencil fraction computation," "manipulating symbols," "memorizing rules or algorithms" and "finding exact forms of answers." In 2006 the NCTM released a new set of standards that partially repudiate the old standards and recognize the importance of basic skills and rules and procedures in mathematics. But the curricula of most states and all the provinces in Canada, and the philosophical viewpoint of most educational consultants I have met, are still based on the old NCTM standards.

When the older standards were released, parents in many states, particularly California, mobilized and formed organizations to oppose NCTM-based curricula. As David Klein recounts in his essay, "A Brief History of American K–12 Mathematics Education in the Twentieth Century," these parents were portrayed by educators and journalists as

> proponents of basic skills, while educational adminis-
> trators, professors of education, and other defenders
> of these programs, were portrayed as proponents of
> conceptual understanding, and sometimes even
> "higher order thinking." This dichotomy is implausi-
> ble. The parents leading the opposition to the NCTM
> standards . . . had considerable expertise in mathe-
> matics, generally exceeding that of the education pro-
> fessionals. This was even more the case of the large
> number of mathematicians who criticized these pro-
> grams. Among them were the world's most distin-
> guished mathematicians, in some cases with mathe-
> matical capabilities near the very limits of human
> ability. By contrast, many of the education profession-
> als who spoke of "conceptual understanding" lacked
> even a rudimentary knowledge of mathematics.

In Canada, mostly in Ontario, some influential math consultants have either banned or tried to ban JUMP in their
school boards because they claim that it does not teach
conceptual or higher-order thinking skills. Many of these
consultants are not aware of the full range of JUMP materials, and many have an incomplete picture of what concepts are and how conceptual understanding emerges in

children (and some are in direct conflict of interest). Because there is so much at stake for children in the educational wars, it is worth examining in detail the confusion surrounding concept.

For some time now educators have advocated that we move away from rote learning of rules and operations. This is a very positive development; students should understand why rules work and how they are connected to the world. But, unfortunately, in arguing against rote learning some educators have set up the false dichotomy between mathematical rules and operations on the one hand and concepts and models on the other. Not all concepts in mathematics are concrete, as the case of negative multiplication illustrates. And if a rule is taught without reference to a model, it is not necessarily taught by rote. Whenever children see a pattern in a rule or apply a rule to a case they have never before encountered, they are doing math conceptually, even if they haven't consulted a model in their work and even if they haven't discovered the rule themselves. The fact that children should also be taught to see the connection between the rule and the model and encouraged to make discoveries doesn't take away from my point.

I once read in a journal for teachers that said when a child uses a rule to find an answer to a problem, the child isn't thinking. I was surprised to learn this, as most of my graduate work in mathematics had consisted of following rules. Many of the rules I learned in graduate school were so deep I doubt I could have discovered their applications on my own (especially not in the five and a half years it took me to get my master's and doctorate). But I was always proud of myself whenever I managed to use one of those rules to solve a problem that wasn't exactly like the examples my professors had worked out on the board. Every time I used a rule to solve a problem I hadn't seen before, I got the distinct impression that I was thinking.

Many teachers and educators have trouble recognizing that following rules involves thought, because they are convinced that students must discover mathematical concepts in order to understand them and because they believe that conceptual always means "having a model" or "being taught from a model." I once showed an influential educator the results of a JUMP pilot that I was very proud of (mentioned in chapter two), in which, after a month of instruction, an entire Grade 3 class (including several slow learners) scored over 90 percent in a Grade 7 test on operations with fractions. When she saw the tests, the educator said they made her blood boil. I explained that many children had shown remarkable improvements in confidence and concentration after completing the unit. I also pointed out that the regular JUMP workbooks do teach the connection between the operation and the model, that the fractions unit is just a brief excursion into the symbolic world of math. But I don't think she heard anything I said. I expect she was so upset because I wasn't supposed to be teaching fractions in Grade 3 without models and, by teaching the children algorithms, I was teaching mathematics that had no conceptual content.

However, children must develop a great many conceptual and higher-order skills even to perform the operations for adding fractions. To see how this is the case, it helps to consider an example. I once came across the following question on a Grade 7 entrance exam for a school for gifted children:

If a ♦ b = a x b + 3, what does 4 ♦ 5 equal?

Most educators would probably say that this is a good conceptual question for Grade 7 students. To solve the problem a student must notice which symbols change and which ones remain the same on either side of the equal sign in the left-hand equation. The letters a and b appear on both sides of the equal sign, but on the right-hand side they are multiplied (then added to the number three). Once the student notices this he or she can see that the solution to the problem is 4 x 5 + 3 = 23. The ability to see patterns of this sort in an equation and to see what changes and what stays the same on either side of an equal sign are essential skills in algebra.

When I teach the JUMP fractions unit, I show students how to add a pair of fractions with the same denominators, by adding the numerators of the fractions while keeping the denominator the same. But then, without further explanation, I ask students how they would add three fractions with the same denominator. In other words, I ask

If 1/4 + 1/4 = 2/4, what does 1/4 + 1/4 + 1/4 equal?

The logical structure of this question is very similar to the question from the enriched entrance exam. To find the answer students have to notice that the number four remains unchanged in the denominators of the fractions and the numbers in the numerators are combined by addition. In my opinion, this question is conceptual in much the same way as the question on the entrance exam is conceptual. Yet the educator whose blood boiled when she saw the fractions unit undoubtedly assumed there was no conceptual content in the algorithms I was teaching.

In the fractions unit children not only learn to pay attention to what changes and what stays the same in an equation or a string of symbols, but they also learn to see and generalize patterns. On almost every page of the unit students must apply a rule they have learned in a particular case to a variety of new cases. The order and patterns in the terms and symbols are constantly varied, and new terms and symbols are always being added. The skills that students develop in the fractions unit—spotting and generalizing patterns and applying rules and procedures—are also called upon and developed every time they apply an operation or an algorithm (such as the long division algorithm I presented in chapter five). Just as infants can develop new cognitive abilities by learning to distinguish subtle variations in the voices, facial expressions and emotions of their caregivers, older children can develop abilities by playing with subtle variations on a pattern or a rule.

In most elementary schools now, children receive very little rigorous instruction that can help them develop an ability to understand or follow a complicated sequence of thoughts. This is because they rarely do any work that requires applying a rule or multi-step procedure, which must be applied differently in different cases or that has any degree of complexity. Many children never really learn to focus or follow a complex train of thought because they are not given enough practice in staying on task, sequencing and performing exercises and activities that would improve their ability to remember and apply the steps of a procedure. Many cognitive abilities are neglected now in the mathematical curriculum, abilities that are as important to higher-order or conceptual thought in mathematics as the ability to construct a concrete model of a problem or invent a new way of carrying out a calculation. They include the ability to see and extend a pattern and to see what changes and what stays the same in an equation or a string of symbols, the ability to follow a procedure or a rule that has a number of steps, the ability to apply a rule to a new case, the ability to recognize which rule should be applied in a particular case, the ability to break complicated tasks down into simple ones, the ability to hold a sequence of steps in memory and the ability to learn and recall facts needed to follow a rule or procedure. All of these abilities can be developed through rigorous practice with rules and algorithms.

Not only do rules and algorithms require a great deal of conceptual and higher-level thought to learn and apply, they also embody a great deal of mathematical content. Standard algorithms such as the algorithm for long division are very elegant shorthand for sequences of physical manipulations or actions (such as dividing up a set of dimes, then exchanging the leftover dimes for pennies). There is no reason why children can't be taught to see the physical actions in the algorithms and to understand and perform algorithms perfectly. In his article, Huang Wu says, "the addition algorithm, like all other standard algorithms, contains mathematical reasoning that would ultimately enhance children's understanding of our decimal number system. Why not consider the alternative approach of teaching these algorithms *properly* before advocating their banishment from classrooms?"

Some educators appear to have accepted the notion that rules and operations are mindless because rules and operations are often learned one step at a time and are only fully mastered after a good deal of practice and application. It is now widely believed in education that a student who only partially understands a mathematical rule or concept, and who can't always apply the concept, extend it to new cases consistently or explain the concept in detail, understands nothing. However, in the days when students were taught operations almost entirely by rote, the majority only partially understood the operations. Some educators who observed this state of affairs concluded that partial knowledge in mathematics is in itself always a bad thing. Rather than simply advocating that people be taught why operations work as well as how they are performed, these educators took the position that if you teach a student how to perform an operation without first teaching all the concepts underlying the operation (or allowing the student to discover the operation), then you will prevent the student from ever properly learning those concepts in the future.

This conclusion is not supported by the actual practice of mathematics. Far from being considered bad, partial knowledge is the daily bread of every practising mathematician. Mathematicians usually start their research by trying to master a small or artificially restricted area of knowledge. Often they will play with simplified systems of rules and operations even before they have devised a physical model for the rules. Ideas seldom arrive full-blown in mathematics: even after a mathematician discovers a new rule or operation, it can take generations before the rule is fully understood. And often it is more the relentless practice with the rule than any physical intuition that allows for emergence of complete understanding.

While partial knowledge isn't necessarily bad, partial success usually is. Even when I introduce kids to ideas that they may only partially understand, I make sure that they are able to complete the exercises I give them. (If students are motivated and confident, I will sometimes let them struggle more with an exercise. They need to learn eventually that it's natural to fail on occasion and that solving problems often takes a great deal of trial and error.) If we applied the standards and methods now used to teach children in elementary schools to graduate students in universities, very few students would ever complete their degree. Children need to be given more practice using rules so they can get used to and gain a complete understanding of them, and they need more guidance when they fail to discover rules by themselves. Rules and concepts are often hard to separate; even in cases where the distinction is clear, mastery of the rules can help induce understanding of concepts as much as understanding of concepts supports mastery of the rules.

Some educators believe that if students are taught how to perform a mathematical operation rather than discovering the method on their own, they are unlikely to ever understand the concepts underlying the operation. The idea that children have to discover an operation to understand it, like many ideas I have encountered in math education, is based on a reasonable idea that has simply been stretched too far. As a teacher I always encourage my students to make discoveries and extend their knowledge to new situations by themselves. But as a mathematician I have a realistic idea what discovery means. I know, from my work as a student and as a researcher, that discoveries in mathematics are almost always made in tiny, painstaking steps.

As I mentioned in chapter three, my best teacher in high school always had us on the edge of our seats during his chemistry lessons. But, though we almost felt as if we were recreating the great discoveries, he didn't expect us to discover the entire periodic table by ourselves. (Of course, if a class is ready to discover the periodic table, then by all means let them discover it. The goal of JUMP is to bring students to a level where they can make interesting discoveries. And I encourage teachers to sometimes assign more difficult, open-ended exercises—as long as students who fail to make discoveries are guided through the material afterwards.)

In the present educational climate teachers seldom verify that all of their students can perform an operation before they assign work that involves the operation. And students are rarely given enough practice or repetition to learn an operation properly. They can easily reach Grade 9 now without anyone noticing that they have failed to discover even the most basic facts about numbers. A teacher who isolates the steps of an operation or procedure and allows students to discover, fully understand and master the steps does not prevent them from achieving conceptual understanding or higher-order thinking. Chess masters don't develop their intuition, their ability to immediately see the best move in a game, by focusing entirely on the big picture or by playing the game. By mastering small sets of moves, studying the games of the masters and memorizing positions, grandmasters are able to develop conceptual abilities that are "near the very limits of human ability."

Mathematicians and writers work in exactly the same way. Repetition and practice don't have to be boring, nor do they have to be rote. If students are encouraged to discover and extend steps by themselves, if they are made to feel that they are meeting a series of challenges and if they are allowed to apply their knowledge to solve interesting problems, they will happily learn even the most challenging operations and procedures. Educational consultants' claims that JUMP teaches children by rote is based on an incomplete picture of how concepts emerge and of JUMP itself. In rote learning, children never learn why a rule or procedure works, nor are they encouraged to discover the rule or the steps of the rule, extend the rule to new cases or discover new rules themselves, as they are in JUMP. In rote learning, teachers do not show children with models and pictures why operations work, nor do they encourage children to discover for themselves the connection between the model and the rule. In rote learning, teachers never show students the big picture or spiral back and forth between the big picture and the small steps. In rote learning, teachers never pay attention to the psychological dimension of teaching and the importance of success, nor do they constantly raise the bar and allow students to show off in front of their peers, as JUMP teachers do. Finally, in rote learning, teachers do not recognize and encourage different approaches to a problem or operation the way JUMP teachers are trained to do.

I believe there will be little progress in education until educators recognize that concepts are complex. The metaphors of the hologram and the anthill more accurately capture the way expertise and comprehension develop in subjects such as mathematics and reading than the misleading dichotomy between higher-order thought and comprehension on the one hand and basic skills, rules and procedures on the other. Teachers can be creative and capable of responding to the diverse needs of their students only if they are not dogmatic or tied to one way of teaching. To reach all students they need to work on all scales—the large and the small—and in all media—the concrete and the symbolic and abstract—rather than being legislated by educational experts and consultants to work almost exclusively on one scale (the large) and in one medium (the concrete). Simplistic pictures and dichotomies in education have led us to neglect the kind of rigorous training and instruction that produces experts. When we accept that concepts are embodied on all scales and in various media, and that understanding can emerge from an accumulation of small conceptual breakthroughs, then we can begin to pay attention to the real barriers that prevent emergent intelligence.

The false dichotomies in education that have become institutionalized in our schools have put up five barriers to learning.

1.By focusing too much on models and assuming that mathematical concepts lie exclusively in models and in the big picture, we have lost sight of how very easy it is for children to learn the individual steps of an operation (such as the addition of fractions) or a procedure (such as rounding) when those steps are isolated and taught one at a time. Even the most brilliant novice chess players need to play variations on a position over and over again before they can see the best move. In mathematics, even very high order thinking skills and problem solving strategies can easily be taught in a rigorous way. I once taught a gifted Grade 8 student some math from a university-level book on computer science. At one point, when the student was stuck on a problem that I had thought would be easy for her, I said "Why don't you just guess and check?" (That is, guess some numbers and try them in the question). The girl replied "Why would I do that? It's useless, it's random, and it could take forever to find an answer." It was clear that even though the girl had spent several years in gifted classes, she had received very little instruction in effective problem solving techniques. I explained to her that she shouldn't guess and check hoping to find an answer to the problem at random: she should guess a few potential solutions to the problem and check to see if they work in order to determine if she has understood the problem correctly and to see if she can spot any potential constraints on the answer, or any patterns in the way her guesses failed to work.

I have seen books that give students lists of strategies that they might use to solve problems (guess and check, work backwards, make a model, try to solve a simpler problem, etc.), but the books themselves do not provide students with enough practice at any one technique to consolidate their understanding of the technique. To give an example of a problem solving strategy: Suppose Ravi is the 122nd person in a line and Carmen is the 256th person in the line. How many people are between them? Many students will simply subtract the number 122 from the number 256 to find the answer. But if students know how to make a simpler version of the problem they will quickly see that this approach does not give the right answer. If Ravi was second in the line and Carmen was fifth, there are actually only two people between them (not five minus two, or three). If you subtract the position numbers of Ravi and Carmen (256-122 = 134) the result is actually one too high so you still have to subtract one from 134 to find the correct answer (i.e. there are 133 people between them). If students were given more extensive and more rigorous practice in various basic problem solving techniques— such as making a simpler version of a problem—they would find math easier and more enjoyable .

2. By focusing too much on the big ideas and on the ends of education we are leaving behind too many students. We

need to look more closely at how textbooks are organized: there are often too many new concepts introduced on one page, too much language, too many barriers to understanding and success. We cannot teach children to communicate by overwhelming them with language, and we cannot teach them to understand different approaches to a subject by teaching them three different explanations before they have mastered one.

3. Expecting children to constantly discover new operations and procedures with little guidance is unrealistic and inefficient. Well-planned discovery-based lessons can be beneficial (especially with stronger classes), but these kinds of lessons need to be balanced with a good deal of rigorous guidance. JUMP has shown that children in Grade 3 can learn to perform operations with fractions flawlessly in less than a month, and that they will ask to stay in during recess for lessons on theoretical computer science. Rather than compelling children to spend so much time playing with blocks and Cuisenaire rods in an attempt to discover standard algorithms or inferior versions of their own, why not guide children through the curriculum as quickly and efficiently as possible, and then allow them to use the tools they have acquired to explore more substantial and more beautiful mathematics?

4. We need to look more closely at the role of memory in mathematics. Some educators seem to assume that a child who discovers an operation or a concept will always find it easy to apply the concept in new situations and will be able to recall the concept immediately, even if he or she hasn't

had an opportunity to think about it for a year. This assumption certainly does not reflect my experience as a mathematician. I discovered original (and rather elementary) algorithms in knot theory that I mastered only after months of practice, but if you were to ask me how one of those algorithms works now, I would have to devote several weeks of hard work to remembering the answer.

Textbooks always include only material that is mandated by the curriculum for a particular grade level. They will often have a single page at the beginning of a chapter with material the student should already have learned, perhaps titled "Do You Remember?" The answer for most students is "No, I don't" or "I didn't learn it properly the first time." The JUMP workbooks are designed to take account of the fact that forgetting is a natural part of learning. In the first workbook for each year we provide extensive scaffolding and reviews that go back about two years.

5. If teachers teach only concepts that students are ready to understand or explain in their entirety, they will not be able to raise the bar incrementally as I described earlier, a method that is key to JUMP's success with weaker students. In Ontario, students in Grade 3 are not expected to add pairs of numbers with more than three digits. I suppose this is because they are not developmentally ready to add larger numbers and because they haven't spent enough time playing with concrete models of large numbers. But I have seen children in Grade 3 classes become very excited when I've challenged them to extend the method for adding three-digit numbers to ten-digit numbers.

Whenever I challenge a class to add larger numbers, I start by teaching students who don't know their addition facts how to add one-digit numbers by counting on their fingers. I make sure the numbers I write on the board are relatively small so that every student has a chance of answering. As I write longer and longer numbers on the board, even the weakest students invariably start waving their hands and shouting, "Oh, oh!" When they succeed in finding the sum of a pair of ten-digit numbers, they think they've conquered Mount Everest.

When Grade 3 students use a rule they have learned for adding three-digit numbers to add ten-digit numbers, they are behaving exactly like mathematicians: they see a pattern in a rule and guess how the rule might work in more complex cases. Children needn't wait until their teacher has purchased the right set of manipulatives or until they are developmentally ready before they can explore their hypotheses.

There is one final barrier to efficiency in teaching that will be far more difficult to remove from our schools, because it is based on centuries of inertia and ignorance. But in my opinion it is the barrier that is causing the most damage in education. That is the topic of the next chapter.

—

CHAPTER SEVEN

COLLECTIVE INTELLIGENCE

—

WHEN MATTHEW WAS FIVE, he had a great deal of trouble buttoning his clothes. His fingers were unable to make the movements required to open a buttonhole and push the button through it, so when he tried to dress himself he would have to give up in frustration. Luckily his parents found an excellent occupational therapist who knew how to reduce the finger movements into a dozen sub-movements that Matthew was able to master one at a time. Now he shows no signs of having once struggled to do up buttons.

Not long after I started tutoring Matthew, his mother said that the methods I used in my lessons reminded her of the exercises he had done with his therapist. I think that comparison is at least partially accurate. When mental tasks are broken into subroutines that can be mastered one at a time, the brain can develop the cognitive capacities required for conceptual thought: the capacity to pay attention or stay on task for long periods, to hold information in the working memory, to see and extend patterns, to draw connections, to make inferences. Just as a hand can be taught to become more dexterous, the brain can be taught to think more fluidly.

Occupational therapy, unfortunately, often requires costly equipment and intensive one-on-one attention, so it is normally very expensive. If schools were required to provide this kind of therapy to all their students they would never be able to balance their budget. But the methods I used to teach Matthew computational and conceptual skills can be used in a classroom, and they cost much less to implement than traditional textbook-based programs. These methods, surprisingly, are even more effective when used with an entire class rather than with one student at a time.

The methods of teaching that I will describe in this chapter are particularly well suited for mathematics, but they can be used in other subjects too. In chapter three I described a lesson in creative writing in which I showed students how to create similes and metaphors that they could use as building blocks for poems. It is possible to teach a lesson in writing, or in subjects such as grammar and reading comprehension, from much more basic starting points. A teacher who attended a JUMP training session told me he used the methods I presented to teach a lesson on grammar. By the end of the lesson his students were so excited they were jumping up to shout out nouns.

The teacher started his lesson with a very simple exercise that all his students could succeed at, and then he started to raise the bar gradually. He first asked his students to give him nouns that fell into very simple categories: "Tell me all the nouns you can think of for something that is big or small." Then he made the categories more difficult, demonstrating how impressed he was when the students answered the harder questions. It is easy to see how teachers could extend this approach: they might ask students to find nouns that fit into two categories—for instance, nouns that name things that are animals and that are big—or nouns that are also verbs. They might even ask students to organize a list of words such as *threw, fly, cat, street* and *hit* into a Venn diagram.

To raise the bar even further, teachers could introduce nouns that are not so obviously also verbs, such as *chair* or *surface,* or they could introduce pronouns and prepositions into the game.

Many adults remember being tortured or confused by tedious grammar exercises at school, so they might have trouble believing that a lesson on nouns could be interesting. But the teacher was able to generate so much excitement around this topic because he understood that the way he structured his lesson and the way he engaged the class as a group were at least as important as the topic he wanted to teach. This is an issue that we have entirely missed in our debates over the curriculum. Those debates almost always revolve around the content of lessons (which facts or concepts should be introduced, and in which order) or around general pedagogical principles (whether the teacher should emphasize the big idea or allow students to discover the concept with concrete materials). But they rarely take into account the psychology of children, of how they behave in groups and how they perceive themselves when they are in groups.

Children have fundamental psychological needs that are far more important than the content of any particular lesson. Children want success: they want to be able to show off to a caring adult, to feel that they are not stupid or inferior to other children, to reach higher levels in an activity (as in a video game), to succeed in front of their peers, to see patterns and play with subtle variations on a theme, to solve puzzles, and to think the same thoughts and experience the same excitement over an idea as other children. Because we have never completely taken into account the things that are deeply important to children—in the planning of lessons, in the development of textbooks and programs, in the way we assess students' work—we have never been able to nurture their intelligence effectively. We need to give children the opportunity to train the way experts do and to practise and solidify their knowledge effortlessly, with joy and excitement.

Even if a teacher used the JUMP methods to teach only some of their lessons in math, I believe the effects would quickly be seen in other subjects: in the students' behaviour, their level of confidence, their ability to focus, their ability to follow a train of thought and make inferences, and their engagement in school. Several informal studies of JUMP, including the pilot in London that I described in chapter four, have suggested that this can happen, as have my observations of many students.

In this chapter I present a problem solving lesson on perimeter to show how easy it is to get to the foundations of any topic in elementary math, and to show how a teacher can structure a lesson so that the fastest students are not bored and the weakest are not left behind. For several reasons, math may well be the easiest subject in which to teach a lesson that has all students working on the same material at roughly the same level. First, it is surprisingly easy to give weaker students the skills and background knowledge they need to keep up in any topic in elementary math, even in highly conceptual or problem solving lessons. Second, it is also easy to assess what students know in math, which is the key to teaching a lesson that engages every student. Third, it is easy to raise the bar for students in math because it is easy to match the size of the step to their abilities. Fourth, it is easy to create bonus questions for faster students without going off topic. One of the most common mistakes teachers make is to give bonus questions that introduce too many new ideas or require too much background knowledge, so they end up spending all their time with the faster students explaining the new material. It is essential to design bonus questions in math that faster students can work on independently.

To understand why the problem solving lesson is effective, it helps to understand why our present methods of teaching children in groups are so inefficient. We fail in a number of ways to take account of children's needs when we put them together in a classroom. Infants would never manage to take their first steps or utter their first words if they were deprived of the constant, loving attention of adults. It is hard to separate infants' capacity to absorb knowledge from their capacity to be adored. Moreover, children don't suddenly turn into stoics or lose their need for unconditional love and attention when they enrol in school at age five or six. However, the conditions under which they are educated change dramatically. They enter a hierarchical system in which only a minority of children ever receive the kind of attention, praise or success that a loving parent can provide. Even as early as Grade 2 or 3 children are able to recognize that certain students are singled out for extra praise or attention, are more successful in the eyes of the teacher, are more intelligent and gifted, and are receiving more of the one tangible reward that school can offer: academic success.

The need for the kind of attention a parent provides never entirely disappears as children get older, even if they develop thicker skins or more difficult personalities. For the girl at the York Detention Centre (in chapter one), it was crucially important that I put checkmarks beside all her questions. And a teacher who used JUMP in a high-security detention centre in Edmonton managed for the first time to get his students to hand in their homework, simply by allowing them to show off in class and be successful.

When teachers single out a few students as successful in a particular subject, it is clear what will happen. Students who consistently receive lower marks or inadequate rewards in the subject, or who are constantly made to feel less successful, gifted or special than another group of students, can do one of two things. They can conclude that either they are stupid or the subject is stupid. It is hard to see how any other outcome is possible, except perhaps in exceptional cases, where by some miracle children develop enough resilience or love of the subject to endure failure and ignore the opinions of their teachers.

If academic or intellectual hierarchies were natural among groups of children and were determined, for instance, by genetic codes or rigid structures in the brain, then the extreme differences that exist among children in every school would be natural. If hierarchies were natural there would be no point in giving false hope or confidence to students who struggle at school. The majority of students would have to learn to cope with being incapable of much success in academic work. But how would we judge our schools if virtually every child who entered school in kindergarten had the potential to learn any subject? How would we judge the methods of instruction used in our schools if, as the research in cognition suggests, almost all children could be trained to develop intellectual and artistic abilities and could become deeply engaged in their work, the way experts are engaged? We would have to admit that there was something wrong with the way we educated our children, because only a small fraction of them in any school would ever do well at or develop a real love for any particular subject.

I believe that children who are educated according to their potential could do well in every subject. I am not claiming that all children will be exactly the same, or that they will all reach the same level of achievement or enjoy every subject equally. The world is complex and exhibits emergent behaviour at every level, so children invariably develop different interests at school and spend more time on activities they like. They will develop different abilities, no matter how similar we make their upbringing and their education. But I believe there is a standard in every subject—well above the one we now expect of competent students—that almost all elementary students could easily achieve.

People fundamentally misunderstand what distinguishes people who do work at the highest level in the arts and sciences from those who are merely competent. It is not a special intellectual gift; at the highest levels of achievement, intelligence is almost secondary. Factors such as passion, confidence, creativity, diligence, luck and artistic flair (even in the sciences) are as important as the speed and sharpness of one's mind. Einstein was not technically a great mathematician, but he had a deep sense of beauty and a willingness to question conventional wisdom. A person's willingness to train relentlessly and to learn in the most efficient manner—by studying and synthesizing the work of other experts—is also a factor in success. The least acknowledged factor in success is undoubtedly luck: many breakthroughs in the arts and sciences occurred because the right combination of ideas happened to fall into the right person's lap. For every breakthrough, often a great many people might have made the advance but were unlucky enough to get beaten to the punch, or were held back by a missing piece of information, faulty data or an invalid presupposition.

Through proper instruction, I believe we could raise the level of virtually all students to the point where they could do well in every subject at school. Of course, whether students would go on to do exceptional work in a particular field would depend on factors beyond the school's control—their level of passion and diligence, their willingness to train efficiently in the subject, even their luck. But schools could control at least one thing: they could educate and inspire students to the point where the majority could choose to follow their passion in virtually any artistic or scientific endeavour.

Why haven't we seen any evidence in our schools to suggest that students could do well in every subject? The evidence has never emerged because we have never created the conditions in our classrooms that would allow it to emerge. The problem is clearly circular. We will never foster emergent intelligence or abilities in weaker students until we remove the psychological and pedagogical barriers that create artificial hierarchies in our schools and prevent weaker students from succeeding. And teachers will never make the effort to remove those barriers until they have seen evidence that emergent intelligence can appear in weaker students. So the hierarchies persist.

The scientific evidence suggests that children are born with roughly equal potential, and that what becomes of them is largely a matter of nurture, not nature. So how does so much potential ultimately disappear in so many children? Why do we observe such extreme differences in students even by Grade 3? Some people believe that children's potential can vanish even before they enter school if they are not properly nurtured in the early years. While I believe this may happen in extreme cases of neglect, the evidence in cognition shows that the brain is plastic beyond the early years, and the results of JUMP suggest that weaker students can make remarkable gains in subjects such as mathematics. I am convinced, as are many teachers who have used JUMP, that the differences that exist between students when they enter school can largely be eliminated or minimized through rigorous training and instruction, to the point where the vast majority of children can work at a very high standard.

But even if teachers believe, as I do, that weaker students can do well at school, their efforts to support these students will not be effective unless they also make an effort to minimize artificial hierarchies in the classroom. It should be clear from the research in cognition why this is the case. The work of neurologists such as Schwartz and Merzenich has shown that the brain can't rewire itself or register the effects of training if it is not attentive. But a child's brain can't be truly attentive unless the child is confident and excited and believes that there is a point to being engaged in their work. The academic hierarchy stands in the way of this because, as

I argued earlier, children who think they are academically inferior to their peers have only two choices: to give up on themselves or to give up on school.

Because the brain does not rewire itself without attention, teachers must do everything they can to focus their students' attention. How a teacher engages the attention of the entire class is as important as the content of the curriculum, and should largely determine how classrooms are organized and the order in which concepts are introduced. I have already argued that students are most focused and attentive when they feel successful. But the level of their attention can be magnified many times when they experience success in front of their peers.

In the nineteenth century the sociologist Emile Durkheim observed a phenomenon in crowds that he called "collective effervescence." According to Durkheim, people's interactions "attain their greatest intensity when they are assembled together and are in immediate relations with one another, when they all partake of the same idea and the same sentiments." The effect he describes may partially account for the success of the JUMP method and the way it works so well at closing the gap between students. When used properly, the JUMP materials are designed to help students "partake of the same idea and the same sentiments." When students work together on the same topic and have a chance to answer the same questions, put their hands up at the same time, work on the same bonus questions and see the solution to a problem at the same time, they experience the collective effervescence that Durkheim described. The effect is particularly striking with students who have never had a chance to show off in public. After the first week of lessons in one class that I visited regularly, a child who had been diagnosed as a selective mute and another who had never raised his hand in class both actively took part in class and always had their hands up. In any class that I have taught for more than a week or two I have generally been able to get every student to participate in lessons.

Last summer I had an opportunity to spend several days with two educators, Dr. Joan Moss of OISE/UT and Dr. Brent Davis of the University of British Columbia (UBC), who are doing very interesting work in children's understanding of algebra and teachers' understanding of mathematics, respectively. Dr. Moss and Dr. Davis spent a good deal of time reviewing the JUMP materials and told me about some research in education and cognition that supports the JUMP methods. (For more information, see Appendix 1.) They also helped me articulate some aspects of how the program works. After watching a video of me teaching the lesson on perimeter, Dr. Davis pointed out several things I did to "engage the collective," as he put it, that I was scarcely aware of. Dr. Davis's term seems a very apt way of describing what teachers should strive to do in their lessons.

One of the most serious barriers to engaging the collective is the idea, widespread among teachers, that math is too deep or difficult to teach to every student in the same way. Only certain students will ever get the big ideas immediately, and if the teacher tries to introduce ideas at a smaller scale, the faster students will get bored and will never go as far as they might. So a teacher has to make a choice between boring and underutilizing the talents of the faster students or losing the weaker students. To demonstrate the inaccuracy of this view, let's look at how a teacher might deliver a problem solving lesson on a fairly advanced topic. The following lesson on perimeter can be done with a whole class in Grade 5 or 6.

A lesson in mathematics can have a narrative or dramatic structure, no matter what the content of the lesson. The teacher can start with an exercise that will invite every student into the lesson (just as a dramatist invites every member of the audience into the story) and allow the teacher to assess what each student knows, so no one is left out of the lesson. I often start a lesson on perimeter with a brief review of the definition of perimeter, and then I will ask the students to copy a simple shape onto grid paper and find the perimeter of the shape (each edge of the grid is one unit long).

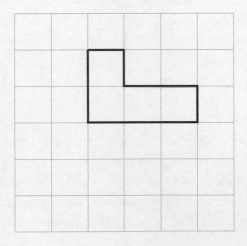

While this exercise might seem so trivial that a teacher could assign it without a second thought, there are barriers to success even in this simple a question. To find the perimeter of a shape, students must be able to add a sequence of numbers. Teachers cannot assume that their students have this skill, even in Grade 5 or 6. But it can take only a few minutes before the lesson starts for the teacher to give weaker students some practice with this skill, even teaching them, if necessary, to add successive numbers by counting up on their fingers. The teacher could give these students a worksheet with boxes where they could keep their running tallies.

$$\boxed{7} \quad \boxed{10} \quad \boxed{11} \quad \boxed{13}$$
$$5 + 2 + 3 + 1 + 2 = \boxed{13}$$

One of the surprising things about elementary and intermediate mathematics—and what makes math an ideal subject for engaging the collective—is that even in fairly interesting or difficult problems, the student needs only a few basic skills or concepts to solve the problem. So, with very little extra effort, a good teacher can always isolate, assess and teach the skills and concepts that weaker students need to keep up in a lesson.

Whenever I work with a class for an extended period of time, I can keep the weakest students moving along with the class by spending ten to fifteen minutes a week working with them in small groups. Many schools have made guided reading lessons a part of the school day so that students get extra practice at reading. Schools could also make guided math lessons standard. Because it is so easy to teach basic skills and concepts in math, these lessons would take on average only a few extra minutes every day, and could be given in small groups while other students worked independently. The students to whom I gave extra help did not feel singled out or inadequate, because they always did well on my tests and were able to participate in class, and I always made sure these students got to answer bonus questions in front of the class.

In the lesson that follows you will notice that students require only two basic skills to solve the problems: they must be able to add sequences of numbers and to perform simple subtractions. There is not a single topic in elementary math in which the teacher cannot quickly get to its foundations and teach weaker students what they need to know to keep up. With a simple question such as the one I assigned, it is easy to overlook another issue of profound importance. In any question, weaker students tend to find certain ways in which to go wrong. When they calculate the perimeter of a shape, for instance, many will miss some sides when they add up the lengths of all the sides. They will often overlook sides with a length of one unit, particularly when two sides of one unit are right next to each other, as in the figure below.

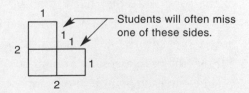

Students will often miss one of these sides.

To make sure that students didn't miss any sides in my lesson, I insisted that they write down the length of each side in their figures. This helped me see that several students were consistently missing sides, and I was able to draw their attention to this right away, so they didn't continue to make the same mistake throughout the lesson.

Paying attention to the small details can make all the difference in a lesson, and will determine whether the teacher engages the entire class or only part of the class. If teachers learn to pay attention to these details they will begin to anticipate where students may be confused or make mistakes. Even the strongest students will make mistakes or misunderstand instructions, but there is very little time for teachers to pay close attention to everyone. They must plan their lessons so that they can assess quickly and consistently what students know. Teachers need to make an effort to spot mistakes or misunderstandings right away, or they will have to spend a great deal of time re-teaching material. Re-teaching material rather than teaching it properly the first time is always inefficient. If the teacher waits too long to correct an error, mistake can be piled upon mistake so that it becomes impossible to know exactly where a student went wrong. And students can become confused and demoralized by making repeated mistakes, losing the level of engagement or the confidence they need to absorb and retain material efficiently. This is why it is so important that teachers know how to break work into steps and introduce ideas incrementally, so they can assess their students' knowledge and provide help at each point in the lesson.

Teachers might wonder how they could possibly make time to assess their students' work while teaching the lesson. The key to keeping track during the lesson of what students know is to present ideas in steps, to assign small sets of questions or problems that test students' understanding of each step before the next one is introduced, and to insist that students present their answers in a way that allows the teacher to spot mistakes instantly. And the teacher should always have a stock of bonus questions ready for students who finish work early.

In the perimeter lesson I drew several extra shapes on the board when I assigned the first question, and I also asked students to make up their own shapes (such as a letter of the alphabet) and find the perimeter. I don't usually expect every student to finish all the questions that I assign on a particular topic; as soon as the weaker students have demonstrated that they understand the essential point of an exercise or have mastered an essential skill, I move on. I don't mark every question that every student answers. When I get to know a class, I spend more time checking the work of students who might need extra help or more encouragement. I sometimes ask the faster students to mark one another's work or make up questions for each other, and often I take up work on the board so I don't have to mark the students' individual papers. But, even if I take up work at the board, I always look over the weaker students' work. Some teachers who have implemented JUMP-style lessons have used educational assistants, special education or resource teachers, interns from teachers' college, parent and community volunteers or even peer tutors to help mark students' work in some of their lessons. The advantage of teaching a lesson in steps is that even volunteers who are not experts in the subject can follow the lesson and help with the marking.

After I assign an initial exercise that will allow weaker students to experience success, I usually introduce some twists and turns in the lesson, just as a writer would in a play. I often create puzzles or challenges for the students to get them more engaged in the lesson. In my perimeter lesson I asked students to make several copies of the shape shown below (left) on grid paper and to find the perimeter of one of the copies. Then I asked students to add a single square to one of the copies, so that at least one edge of the added square was joined to an edge on the original figure, but so that edges didn't only partially overlap. I showed them an example of where they might add the square.

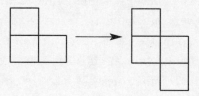

When you add a square to a figure you would expect its perimeter to increase, which is exactly what students found when they added a square in the position I showed them: the perimeter of the first figure is eight and the perimeter of the second is ten. But then I told the students I had a puzzle for them. There is exactly one place where you can add a square to the original figure and the perimeter will stay the same. I knew some students would solve this puzzle very quickly, so I also challenged them to find a place where they could add a square to the shape below so that the perimeter would actually decrease (try to find it!).

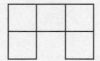

When I give this kind of lesson on perimeter I sometimes ask students to explain how adding the square causes the perimeter to stay the same or decrease. I give stronger classes additional puzzles such as the following: starting with a single square and adding one square at a time, could you ever build a figure with a perimeter that is an odd number?

My goal in the perimeter lesson was to get students to solve some problems where they would be given the perimeter of a shape and the length of some of the sides, and they had to deduce the length of the remaining sides. The work I did in the early part of the lesson was intended to give me time to assess whether all the students could find the perimeter of a shape and to get the students excited about solving problems. To prepare the students for the problems on finding the missing length, I asked them if they could draw a rectangle with a perimeter of twelve units (using sides whose lengths were whole numbers). After the students had spent a few minutes trying this, I asked them how many different rectangles they could find with a perimeter of twelve units. There are three:

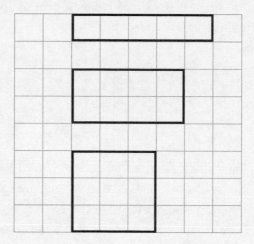

When the students finished this exercise I asked them to repeat it using figures with a perimeter of eighteen units and then twenty-two units. I challenged them to tell me how they could organize their work so they would be sure to find all the possible solutions. Many students saw that they could use the order of natural numbers to organize their work: they could start with a rectangle one unit wide and find the missing length, then a rectangle with a width of two units and so on.

I then asked the students to solve the following puzzle: suppose you have a rectangle with a perimeter of fourteen units and a width of two units. What is the length of the other sides? I assigned several other puzzles of this sort, and also asked students to find the side-lengths of squares that had perimeters of twelve units, twenty units and one hundred units, respectively. Some interesting things happened in the lesson at this point. Even the weaker students in the class, who had initially made mistakes when they were calculating the perimeter of simple figures, were able to solve the problems, and some of those students volunteered to explain to the class how they got their answers. Students came up with several ingenious ways of finding the missing lengths, which I let them explain to the class. If I hadn't spent so much time assessing and encouraging the weaker students at the beginning of the lesson, and if I hadn't given them warm-up problems that required drawing various rectangles with fixed perimeters, those students wouldn't have been able to participate in the more difficult part of the lesson.

After the students had told me how they found the missing lengths of the rectangles, I said I would give them a challenge. I drew a rectangle on the board and wrote the width— five units—on one of the sides. I told the students that the perimeter was thirty units and challenged them to find the missing length. I purposely chose numbers that looked harder but were easy to add and subtract, so that all the students would have a chance to answer the question. Because they had been so successful with their previous work, even the students who had initially made mistakes were anxious to answer the question. I continued to raise the bar, using numbers that were multiples of ten so everyone could do the calculations. When I drew a rectangle with a side-length of two hundred and told the students its perimeter was one thousand, they started standing up at their desks and saying "Oh, oh!" as they waved their hands in the air. (One student got so excited she set herself the problem of finding the side-length of a square with a perimeter of one thousand.) I then assigned the students several harder problems in which they had to deduce missing information to solve the questions, and I ended the lesson by drawing the following shape on the board and challenging them to find the missing sides and the perimeter.

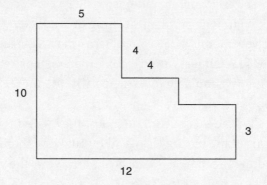

I was able to cover all of this material in a forty-five-minute lesson. I didn't bore the faster students, and the weaker students were able to participate right up to the end of the lesson. And this was not an easy class; it was an inner-city school, and there was a two- or three-grade level difference between the students. I didn't know the students in the class at all, so I had to spend a fair amount of time at the beginning of the lesson making sure the weaker students could find perimeters (if it had been my class I would have coached the weaker students before the lesson). But I still managed to cover a great deal of material without leaving anyone behind. In classes that I have taught for longer periods, where I could spend more time assessing and helping the weaker students, I have been able to build real momentum in my lessons.

A Grade 3 class that I taught for five weeks learned an enormous amount on fractions, and all of them ended up getting over 90 percent on a Grade 7 test. By assessing and paying attention to their weakest students, teachers can not only cover more material in a lesson, they can also change the atmosphere in their classes, and may even change many of their weaker students beyond recognition. After a week or so, all of the students in the Grade 3 class would wave their hands to answer questions and would beg to come up to the board so they could show off their work. By the third week I was often unable to predict who would finish a worksheet first. One student, who had been diagnosed as a slow learner, finished his final exam before half of the class and earned a mark of 92 percent.

A teacher in Vancouver, who had recently observed a Grade 5 class in which JUMP principles had been rigorously applied for several months, told me how surprised she was at what she saw. More than half of the students had been designated as having learning disabilities, but the teacher said she hadn't been able to tell which ones they were. Even though the lesson ran from 9:00 a.m. until 10:30 a.m., all the students were engaged for the entire lesson. Many educators who have used JUMP or observed

JUMP classes have said how surprised they were at the performance of the weaker students. The report from London that is on the JUMP website and the surveys of teachers that I mentioned in chapter three have confirmed how well weaker students can do when they are given a chance.

Engaging the collective is not simply a matter of fairness; it is also a matter of efficiency. While the idea may seem counterintuitive, teachers will enable their faster students to go further if they take care of the slowest students. Teachers can create a real sense of excitement about math in the classroom simply by convincing the weaker students that they can do well at the subject. The class will cover far more material in the year and stronger students will no longer have to hide their love of math for fear of appearing strange or different.

There will always be differences in ability and motivation among children, but those differences (particularly in speed) would probably not have much bearing on long-term success in mathematics if school were not so intent on making differences matter. Because children's level of confidence and sense of self will largely determine what they learn, teachers can easily create artificial differences among them by singling out some as superior and others as inferior. I've learned not to judge students too hastily; I've seen many slower students outpace faster students as soon as they were given a little extra encouragement or help.

The advantages of engaging the entire class and allowing students to work on roughly the same material at the same time are obvious. The experience of working collectively channels the attention of weaker students so that new abilities begin to emerge in those students and differences between students are minimized. Students who work collectively do not passively soak up knowledge; they become actively engaged in solving problems, both for the joy of solving the problem and also for the joy of presenting their answers in front of the class. Students can work at their own pace and can find their own level with a problem (there are always bonus questions for students who finish work early), but none feel they are being left behind. The teacher can assess the work of every student and can immediately help students who make mistakes or misunderstand material, because the steps in the work have been isolated and taught effectively and because the students are all working on the same material (as opposed to group work, where students are often working on many different things at many different levels). Artificial hierarchies are neither created nor emphasized, and students are always challenged to show off and move to higher levels, so they become deeply engaged in their work and teachers do not have to deal with disruptive behaviour from students who have been left behind. Because students feel they are being equally rewarded by the teacher, they work not to be better than their peers but rather to get to higher levels in their own work, to solve more interesting or challenging problems. Students thus develop a healthier engagement in their work and a healthier attitude towards their peers.

I would not, of course, recommend that teachers teach all lessons in the style I have presented. Such lessons require a good deal of energy, and children will also benefit from working on projects individually or in small groups and circulating between activity centres in a classroom. Teachers should sometimes teach more open-ended lessons, in which students can take the lesson in whatever direction they are inspired to explore. And teachers will sometimes want to allow their students to struggle more. I recently watched a wonderful lesson at the Institute for Child Studies (ICS) at OISE/UT during which the teacher pretended to be confused about fractions. The students were also confused at first, but after working their way through their misconceptions they became more and more excited about correcting their teacher. The most effective mix of lessons for a class will likely vary depending on the level of the class and the tastes and talents of the teacher. But if students are able to work collectively in many of their lessons, and if teachers are careful to assess and help their weaker students consistently so that differences are not created or unnecessarily emphasized, I believe children could go much further and have much more fun at school. Teachers would likely end up doing much less work in the long run and would find teaching much more enjoyable, because they would not have to be constantly re-teaching material or dealing with the disruptive behaviour that stems from failure.

ENGAGING THE COLLECTIVE

If teachers are to improvise in a lesson and take it in new directions according to what students discover and get excited about, and if they are to recognize when students' work is correct (even if they solve a problem a different way) or when students are confused, they must know their material well. But many elementary school teachers are not well trained in math, and some are even afraid of it. I have given professional development sessions in two schools in the past year where not a single teacher could correctly answer a question on ratios and percents from the Ontario provincial Grade 6 exam.

Many boards offer professional development sessions in which teachers are shown interesting activities with math or approaches to problem solving lessons, usually involving concrete materials or games. But while this kind of training can be beneficial, it is clearly not adequate for teachers who do not have a strong background in math. Teachers need a resource that will show them, in very simple terms and in a step-by-step manner, how to break into their component parts the various skills and concepts in mathematics for every curriculum requirement. And teachers need to be shown different ways of solving problems, another reason why I developed the JUMP workbooks and why JUMP is developing online training.

Teaching in a way that engages the whole class requires constant assessment. To assess students effectively, teachers must know how to break their material into steps so they can see where students are having trouble and provide remediation. Teachers are not usually trained to work at this minute level of detail, and they are not supported in this kind of work by traditional texts. To give an example, if you ask a student in Grade 4 how far apart the dots are in the diagram below, many students will start counting the distance between the dots by putting their finger on the first dot and counting that step as "one."

HOW SOME CHILDREN WILL COUNT INCORRECTLY

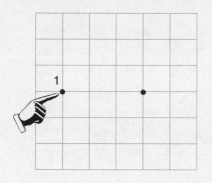 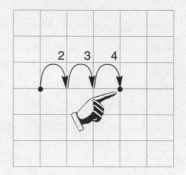

In a large class teachers will not be able to tell if some of their students are counting incorrectly unless they have some means of assessing this. But if teachers can't verify that students are counting correctly there is no point in beginning the lesson. The JUMP workbooks contain a number of exercises in which students simply say how far apart two dots are (horizontally or vertically) so teachers can see immediately if a student is counting correctly. I have never seen a traditional text that helps teachers properly assess whether their students have the basic skills they need to start a lesson, which is why I developed the JUMP workbooks.

I have a rather radical idea about the way we should assess students, which I hope could be tested properly one day. The idea is based on my observations of adults and teenagers who once struggled with mathematics when they were in school. I have taught many adults and teenagers who told me they were hopeless at math, including many who dropped out of math in Grade 10. It usually takes me only a couple of hours to teach these people to understand fractions completely, so that they can perform operations with fractions perfectly and can even explain with a model why all the operations work. From what I have observed, I am convinced that if people live in the world long enough, and if they do not have any severe perceptual or intellectual disabilities, they will naturally gain enough experience to understand every aspect of elementary math, and even higher levels of math.

If children were not continually confused and made to feel inferior in math, and if they were guided properly at school, they would eventually—even at a fairly early age—develop a complete understanding of the elementary curriculum. But complete understanding will naturally develop at different ages in different students. For instance, some students will almost certainly develop the ability to explain how they found their answers to questions and to communicate their understanding of concepts, at a later age than other students, since this ability depends on other abilities, including the ability to communicate in whatever language is being used in the classroom.

I believe we would do a better job of nurturing the natural growth of understanding in students if we used two kinds of assessment in our schools, one visible and the other invisible. In the visible form of assessment, students would receive marks on the things that teachers guaranteed they could teach all children, or virtually all children, at a particular age. There is no reason, for instance, that children could not be taught number facts and basic operations with numbers at a very early age; the results of JUMP have demonstrated this. But the marks would represent neither a ranking nor punishment for not succeeding. They would be a reward for the student's work and verification that the school had done a proper job of teaching the subject.

In the visible form of assessment all students would receive roughly the same marks. There might be two marks—for instance, A and possibly A+ for students who have done extra work—and a class would not move on until all, or virtually all, the students had received a satisfactory mark. This scheme is certainly not unrealistic, considering that inner-city Grade 3 students can score more than 90 percent on Grade 7 tests after only several months of JUMP instruction.

In the invisible form of assessment, teachers would keep track of all the things students need to know to completely understand various concepts. These records would be passed on from grade to grade and a summary would be given to parents (with a request that they not reveal the contents to their children without very good reason). Teachers would not use the records to make students feel inadequate, to rank them or to pick out those unlikely to ever properly learn a subject. They would use them to find out where students might need extra practice or reinforcement of skills or concepts and to constantly nurture their understanding (which would eventually emerge as they acquired more experience in the world—as I have seen with my older students).

Children must eventually learn to deal with failure, and they must learn that some problems take an enormous amount of effort to solve. Even if schools were to use the forms of assessment I have described, they would still have to provide students with opportunities to struggle and sometimes even fail. But students would likely be more resilient and able to endure the hardship if they had a background of success and affirmation in their early years. And the gains students would make from learning and succeeding collectively, and from not always being ranked and made to feel like failures, would almost certainly allow schools to set the standards of visible assessment far above their present standards.

Putting on a performance that will engage an entire class is something of an art, but an art that teachers can easily learn. Any teacher can apply some extremely simple principles in the classroom that can make an enormous difference to weaker students. For instance, studies in education have suggested that if teachers wait a few seconds after they have asked a question and allow students time to think, rather than choosing the first student to put a hand up, students learn more and participate more in lessons. As well, if teachers present examples with easier numbers even when they are raising the bar (as I did in the perimeter lesson), weaker students will have a chance to show off. If teachers always make an effort to include all the students in a lesson, they will quickly develop other strategies for engaging their class.

If they wish to engage the whole class, teachers will not always be able to start with the big idea, and they will sometimes have to work symbolically rather than with models, since symbols are much easier for some students to work with. Students will have do a good deal of individual work, which must be constantly assessed by the teacher, so that every individual can truly be part of the collective. Students need certain skills to keep up with other members of their class, and they must be given enough individual practice and training at those skills, otherwise the teacher will lose the collective.

If students were to receive with some degree of consistency the kind of instruction I have described in this chapter, I believe we could create the kinds of schools that philosophers such as Dewey dreamed of, where children would be actively engaged in making discoveries and extending their knowledge. But the methods required to engage the collective go against the grain of current educational practice. And many barriers in education stand in the way of this kind of work.

———

CHAPTER EIGHT

WORDS FALLING LIKE SNOW: ORWELL'S WARNING

———

BY THE END OF THE SEVENTEENTH CENTURY, the astronomers of Europe had a great many reasons to be proud of the state of their profession. Newton's newly discovered laws of motion, along with an array of new instruments such as the telescope, allowed them to track the movements of the planets and stars so precisely that they could predict many celestial events to the nearest minute or hour. And the laws they relied on to make their predictions were universal: they applied equally to the smallest meteorite and the largest and most distant star. But the astronomers were bothered by a fact that was admittedly rather trivial compared to the vast scale of the universe or the scope of their scientific achievements. Newton's laws could not account for the motion of a single, somewhat inconsequential heavenly body. Io, the innermost moon of Jupiter, was supposed to complete its orbit in forty-two and a half hours. But Io never seemed to stick to the schedule preordained by the laws. When Io disappeared behind Jupiter something odd would invariably happen: the moon would either slow down or speed up, apparently at random, so that no one could say precisely when it would reappear.

In 1676, a full decade before Newton published his theory of gravitation, a twenty-one-year-old Danish scientist named Ole Rohmer found a simple way to account for Io's strange motions. But his solution to the puzzle would not gain wide recognition until almost a century later. Astronomers in Rohmer's day believed that the speed of light was either infinite or so great it could never be measured. In calculating the moment at which a heavenly body should appear at a particular spot in the sky, astronomers assumed that they could safely ignore the time it took light to travel from the body to Earth.

The belief that light travels at infinite or near infinite speed, held by all the astronomers at the renowned Paris Observatory where Rohmer worked as an assistant, was based on a single experiment that had been carried out in the mid-1600s. Following a suggestion by Galileo, Italian scientists had tried to measure the time it took light to travel between two hilltops in Florence. But even though the hilltops were a mile apart, the technology of the day was far too primitive to discern any difference between the time the light left one hilltop and when it arrived at the other.

Rohmer demonstrated that Io's motions could easily be accounted for if light travelled at a speed of approximately

670,000,000 miles per hour (astonishingly close to the best current estimate). He realized that, when Earth was farther away from Jupiter, light from Io would take longer to reach it, so the moon's reappearance would seem to be delayed. In the summer of 1676 Rohmer accurately predicted that, on November 9 of the same year, Io would appear approximately five minutes later than the leading models predicted.

Rohmer's career in the sciences proved to be about as brief as the time light takes to travel from Jupiter to Earth. Not content to circulate his prediction among his esteemed colleagues at the observatory, he announced it publicly, at a scientific conference, as a challenge to the observatory's director. In spite of the astonishing accuracy of Rohmer's prediction and the tenuous nature of the evidence on which the director's theories were based, the astronomers at the observatory, and in Europe as a whole, still refused to accept that light moved at a measurable speed. They pointed to other factors that would explain Rohmer's prediction, including some hypothetical clouds in Jupiter's upper atmosphere that might produce a distorting haze. Rohmer quickly went from being a promising young astronomer in Paris to working as a highway inspector in Denmark.

The kind of treatment that Rohmer received from his colleagues for advancing a new idea is still commonplace in the sciences today. Even in the most rigorous fields of research, people can be irrational or arrogant or can succumb to peer pressure or the urge for self-promotion. Scientists often have blind spots that make them prone to error. It is not hard to find examples of otherwise brilliant researchers who have clung to an idea in the face of contradictory experimental data, because it was too hard to admit that a younger scientist was correct or because the majority of their colleagues, or a more powerful colleague, believed in the idea. In his book *The Structure of Scientific Revolutions,* Thomas Kuhn points out that paradigm shifts in science often occur only after an entire generation of older scientists who stubbornly resisted change has retired or died.

To mitigate against the human tendency towards irrational or self-serving thought, scientific journals have developed rigorous standards of publication. Papers accepted by journals generally undergo extensive screening by referees. Exacting standards for the design of experiments and for making logical and statistical inferences have been established in the hard sciences—medicine, physics, biology, chemistry, mathematics—so that even when incorrect results are published, the errors are often quickly discovered. This system of checking results is vitally important in the sciences. Scientists simply don't have time to verify that all the theories on which their work is based are correct; they rely on the integrity of the peer review system, so that whenever they cite another scientist's result, they are confident in the soundness or validity of that result.

It is doubtful that anyone doing research in education would claim that the standards of investigation and of peer review in their field are as rigorous as the standards that apply to research in the sciences. But that doesn't mean there isn't good work being carried out by academics in educational faculties. I have had the opportunity to work with a number of math educators at OISE/UT, ICS, UBC and the University of Western Ontario who are doing extremely interesting work; they helped me articulate some of the principles behind the JUMP method, learn new methods and improve the JUMP workbooks and teacher's guides. I have also read many articles in education journals that have contained helpful ideas on lessons and different styles of teaching. Some papers in education do meet high standards of experimental rigour, and as long as one doesn't confuse the bulk of research in education with research in the hard sciences (or underestimate how difficult it is to make generalizations and predictions about children that will hold for all children), there is much to be learned from it.

Academic papers that are published in any field, even in the arts, are commonly referred to as research papers. When administrators and consultants in school boards and education ministries draw conclusions about educational practice based on research papers in education, they must be careful not to be confused by the broad application of the term "research." These papers, like those in the sciences, generally support their claims by referring to other papers in the field. But the purpose of citations in educational papers is not entirely clear. An author who writes a research paper in English literature will often cite another paper to give credit for an idea. In educational papers, however, citations play a more ambiguous role. Many authors appear to make citations to prove the validity of their claims by appealing, for instance, to the results of an experiment or the authority of other authors. But as educators will admit themselves, many educational papers fail to meet the basic standards of logical and experimental rigour that are required of scientific papers. This makes the whole edifice of educational theory somewhat shaky, as it is not clear how much weight citations actually carry.

The mathematician Herbert Wilf wrote an excellent paper on this issue titled "Can There Be 'Research in Mathematical Education'?" Wilf looked closely at a number of articles that had been recommended to him as exemplary. In one article, which was published in the NCTM *Journal for Research in Math Education (JRME)*, the authors claimed that the educational reforms proposed by the NCTM, implemented in many schools in the early nineties, were having a significant positive effect on academic achievement in math. According to the paper, "Current evidence from existing research projects that were instigated prior to, or coinciding with, the release of the reform documents indicate that students in reform-based classes do have significantly better achievement in mathematics than those in traditional instruction."

Wilf examined the three citations that the authors of the paper used to support their claim. He found that the first paper cited contained a serious flaw in its experimental design. The second paper was based on reasonably sound design but found no statistically significant difference in academic achievement between a group of students who had received reform-based instruction and a control group. The third article contained no statement that looked like a conclusion except for this sentence: "To summarize, the data suggests that teaching and learning can be related through the kinds of instructional tasks provided and the nature of the classroom discourse." As Wilf says, "If I didn't miss something, what that says is that teaching and learning can be related to what goes on in the classroom." Well, I certainly hope so. As Horatio said to Hamlet, "There needs no ghost, my lord, come from the grave, to tell us this."

Poorly designed experiments in education often violate what Wilf calls "one of the most elementary and fundamental principles of randomized trials: thou shalt not self select." In the flawed experiment that Wilf discusses, two groups of teachers were selected to teach math to Grade 2 students. One group used traditional methods and the other used a program that, according to the article, was "generally compatible with a socioconstructivist theory of knowledge and recent recommendations of the NCTM." In the experiment a great deal of care was taken to ensure that the students were randomly assigned to the classes. But, as Wilf points out,

> The classes that followed the NCTM reform model, the "test group," in other words, were taught by teachers who volunteered to do so. That means that those teachers were the kind of people who are receptive to change and to trying something new. That makes the teachers who taught the control group the non-reform curriculum, a group of non-volunteering sorts of teachers: just the kind that you might expect not to be so good at inspiring the young with the beauties of mathematics. In other words, the instructors were self selected to match the division of

groups; a classical violation of the most elementary principles of the design of such experiments.

Authors of educational papers will sometimes draw conclusions that don't strictly follow from their data, even if the data are sound. The most common error of this sort involves what I would call the "argument from past failures." A paper will cite some past teaching practice that was not particularly successful—for example, rote teaching of standard algorithms—and then claim that the only alternative is the method of teaching that the paper supports. To give an example, I once read a paper that cites studies showing that many children and adults can't do computations with large numbers and many don't understand the algorithms they were taught for performing those operations. Considering the way math was taught when I went to school, this news didn't surprise me. But the conclusion the author makes from her observations did. Rather than recommending that schools do a better job of teaching operations, the author draws a conclusion similar to one that many other educators have advocated. They claim the data show that standard methods for operations should not be emphasized in schools; instead, children should be encouraged to develop their own methods of computation.

I certainly agree with the author that children should be encouraged to develop various non-standard tricks and "mental math" strategies for computation (and if they fail to discover these strategies they should be taught them). But it is important to bear in mind that entire civilizations failed to discover the idea of zero as a place-holder for operations such as addition and division. If the Romans couldn't develop an effective method of division over the course of eight centuries (just try dividing large numbers using Roman numerals!), it seems unrealistic to expect children to discover a great deal on their own. And if schools have failed to teach algorithms well in the past, that does not imply that they cannot do so now. Using the methods that I presented in chapters five and seven, it is possible to teach even challenged students to apply and understand standard algorithms.

Sometimes the argument from past failures is used somewhat deceptively, as in the following passage: "Performance in many of the indicators related to fractions and decimals is not as strong as might be expected based on provincial curricula. This implies that, for many students, perhaps the curriculum related to these topics at these particular grade levels should be approached as an exploration—certainly concretely or contextually—rather than for the purpose of expecting mastery." The author clearly would like to claim that the failure of students to perform well with fractions and decimals "implies" that her approach (the teaching of fractions through "explorations" and not putting so much emphasis on mastering operations) should be adopted. However, that inference is invalid. The fact that students are not doing well with fractions and decimals does not imply that any particular approach must be adopted; it implies only that present methods of teaching these topics aren't working. Note that the author carefully adds "perhaps." When "perhaps" and "implies" are placed next to each other they form a nonsensical phrase. The author might have used "suggests," but then her argument would not appear to carry the logical force of implication.

Educators will sometimes make sweeping generalizations based on rather limited results. The paper "Interference of Instrumental Instruction in Subsequent Relational Learning" by Dolores Pesek and David Kirshner (2000) has been widely cited by educators as showing the harmful effects of teaching rules and procedures before teaching concepts. Steve Leinwand and Steve Fleishman claim, for instance, that "in the existing research, students who learn rules before they learn the concepts tend to score significantly lower than do students who learn concepts first," and they cite Pesek and Kirshner's paper as the "most convincing" piece of research on this issue. Susan Brown, Antoinette Seidelmann and Gwendolyn Zimmermann also claim that "the Pesek and Kirshner study clearly illustrates the potentially detrimental effect of teaching for procedural knowledge prior to teaching for conceptual knowledge."

The study in question, which was conducted under limited circumstances (over a period of eight days with several Grade 5 classes), actually found no significant difference on test scores between students who were taught procedures for finding area and perimeter before they were taught the concepts, and a group of students who were simply taught the concepts. By conducting interviews with the students, the authors found that those in the procedural group were more likely to have misunderstood the concepts, but the most they could conclude from their experiment was that those in the procedural group "achieved no more and probably less conceptual understanding" than the other group.

Even if Pesek and Kirshner had found more striking differences between the groups in their study, the study should not carry as much weight as it does because no serious educator who thinks that rules and procedures should be taught rigorously would recommend teaching them in the way they were taught in the experiment. Students in the procedural group were given formulas for area and perimeter with no explanation and were asked to do rather tedious calculations with the formulas. As Pesek and Kirshner say, "at no time were formulas justified." While I have argued that children can learn conceptual skills (such as sequencing and pattern recognition) by following rules and procedures, I also recommend that teachers allow students to discover the steps of the rule, to see patterns in and extend the rules, and that they constantly spiral back and forth between rules, procedures and models. Even in the fractions unit, which is the most procedural of the JUMP units, I recommend that teachers use illustrations to show students why the rules work. But most importantly, I recommend that teachers use the teaching of rules and procedures for positive psychological effect. In the experiment, the teachers delivering the procedural lessons did little to make the lessons interesting: they did not try, for instance, to raise the bar or challenge the students to extend the rules to new cases. Instead students were asked to write the formulas for area and perimeter repeatedly before they applied them, as they might have to do in a detention. The most the authors could have proved by teaching rules using this method is that if you give children uninteresting work and prevent them from exercising their minds and if you avoid teaching teach them any concepts when you teach the rules, they will likely have a harder time learning concepts later than if they hadn't been taught any math at all.

There are some teachers who, unfortunately, teach math simply by dictating sets of formulas to their students. Students would certainly benefit if educators were to cite Pesek and Kirshner's study to encourage such teachers to do a better job teaching rules. But educators will sometimes cite such research to attack educational programs that advocate that rules and procedures be taught rigorously. Brown, Seidelmann and Zimmermann, for instance, criticize Wu (whom I mentioned in chapter six), but his position is painted as advocating that teachers teach "definitions, symbols and isolated skills in an expository manner without first focusing on building deep, connected meaning to support those concepts." These authors seem to have missed one of Wu's points, as he shows clearly how to teach a number of algorithms so that students have mastery as well as deep conceptual understanding of the algorithms.

A growing number of educational researchers and psychologists have begun to challenge the research that has been used to justify programs that are now established in North American schools. Cognitive scientists, such as the

Nobel laureate Herb Simon, have argued that programs based on constructivist ideas are not supported by research in cognition, (see Appendix 1 for papers on this issue). In 1999 the state board of education in California contracted a group of educational researchers and cognitive scientists to review and locate "high-quality research" about achievement in mathematics: "From a total of 8,727 published studies of mathematics education in elementary and secondary schools, the research team identified 956 experimental studies. Of those, 110 were deemed high-quality research because they met tests of minimal construct and internal and external veracity." In the United States two hundred mathematicians, including several Fields medalists, took out an advertisement in the *Washington Post* to deliver an open letter to the U.S. secretary of education. The letter petitioned education authorities to stop recommending certain math programs and textbooks and the mathematicians based their objections on the educational research that claimed to support those programs. And, as I noted earlier, even the NCTM, whose journal published some of the research the mathematicians took issue with, has now revised the position it took in the nineties and is recommending a more balanced approach to math education, with more emphasis on number facts and standard algorithms. This change of stance should serve as a warning to anyone who considers educational research to be a science; a great deal of the educational research published in the past fifteen years claims to have shown that previous NCTM standards were best practices.

When educational research claims to have proven defini-tively that certain methods of teaching are best practices, education suffers. People are seldom more destructive than when they invent simple theories to solve complex prob-lems. In education there are too many variables to control for a researcher to prove that one method of teaching or one philosophy is necessarily, under all conditions, superior to another. Well-controlled experiments in education can cer-tainly point to approaches that school boards might want to try, but it is always best to retain a degree of humility and a sense of balance in talking about best practices.

Given that education is not a hard science, it is clearly not wise to take educational theory as the gospel truth, particu-larly when educational researchers don't always use rigorous methods of experimentation and argument and there is still conceptual confusion in the field, often based on the misuse of language I discussed in chapter four. But school boards and education ministries across Canada now rely heavily on the results of educational research and the advice of educa-tional experts in setting curricula and evaluating textbooks. Some administrators and educational consultants I have met behave as though the theories behind the programs they are selling or promoting have been proven with the same degree of rigour as the most well-established results in mathematics and physics.

A little over a year ago I attended a conference on research in math education. The participants in the workshop I had been assigned to were asked to introduce themselves and say a little about their background. I had barely begun to talk about my work with JUMP when a math consultant employed by a school board, who also teaches pre-service teachers at a university, interrupted me to say that Piaget's theories and brain-based research had proven that JUMP can't work. I said that in my opinion there was some question about the validity of those theories, particularly when they were applied in education. I also asked the consultant if she was aware of the full scope of the JUMP program—we had recently developed a great deal of new material, including problem solving lessons and lessons using concrete materials, that no one had seen except JUMP staff and some teachers who advise us. After some discussion I suggested that if the consultant believed in doing research, she would surely want to test ideas that were different from prevailing ideas. Why not, I suggested, run some JUMP implementations in her board and see for herself whether there was anything useful in the program? She replied, "We couldn't do anything that would harm children." This exchange might have been amusing if it hadn't been for what followed. Last summer two highly respected researchers in math education in Canada, backed by funding from a ministry of education, approached the school board where the consultant worked to see if they would be interested in running an experimental JUMP pilot. The pilot was blocked by the math consultants in the board.

In any given field and in any given era, there are always received beliefs—like the belief that light travels at an infinite or immeasurable speed—that will be accepted by the majority of people working in the field. Right now educators and consultants in school boards, ministries and faculties of education tend to espouse the kinds of theories I discussed in chapters three to seven of this book. The math programs, curricula and textbooks that are now in use in school boards across Canada were deeply influenced by research in math education. Ministry documents are now heavily footnoted or laced with quotes from educational papers. I believe this is a very dangerous trend in education: some of this research is now being widely disputed even by math educators. It is important to allow other ideas to be tested.

There is one danger in relying too much on research that most people are unaware of. In the pharmaceutical industry, checks and balances have been established to ensure that research isn't unduly influenced by companies that will gain or lose money based on the research results. In fact, many people think that controls in the pharmaceutical industry aren't strong enough. But the controls in education are virtually nonexistent. Many educators employed by faculties of education or by school boards and ministries receive funding from textbook companies for their research, or they derive income from those companies as authors and consultants.

I don't think it is an accident that the curriculum in Canada now demands that kids in Grade 7 do much of their work with fractions using concrete materials. There may not be any conspiracy involved, but you can see how this state of affairs might have come about. Textbook companies now either directly sell the various fraction strips, grids and blocks that kids must use to add fractions or they are owned by companies that sell those materials. Over time those companies would tend to provide funding or offer consulting fees or royalties to educators who support the use of the materials they sell.

If education is not a hard science, what role should educational research play in the school system? It is not hard to see one very clear role that papers in education can play. The best papers that I've read have offered interesting suggestions for lessons or new ways of looking at what goes on in schools and classrooms. Clearly one role that education researchers can play in the school system is to inform and inspire their readers. But if educators hope to communicate new and inspiring ideas, they must have a deep understanding of and respect for the medium they use to communicate those ideas.

In the essay "Politics and the English Language" (which should be required reading for students of education, and students in the social sciences), George Orwell warned that the English language at the time of the Second World War was in "a bad way." To make his point he rewrote an elegant biblical passage in more modern terms. Here is the original passage:

> I returned and saw under the sun, that the race is not to the swift, nor the battle to the strong, neither yet bread to the wise, nor yet riches to men of understanding, nor yet favour to men of skill; but time and chance happeneth to them all.

And here is Orwell's improvement:

> Objective consideration of contemporary phenomena
> compels the conclusion that success or failure in com-
> petitive activities exhibits no tendency to be commen-
> surate with innate capacity, but a considerable ele-
> ment of the unpredictable must invariably be taken
> into account.

I have reproduced some examples of educational writing
below to show a style of writing that is common in education
today. I took these examples from a variety of books and
articles in my own collection. I didn't make any great effort
to find these examples; for the most part I simply opened
some texts at random and wrote down whatever caught my
eye. I didn't try to find writing that was particularly bad,
although one or two of the passages would qualify as that.
Although the writing in some passages is better than in
others, all of them have some features in common that are
found in a good deal of writing about education.

> The role for current theories of learning and teaching
> is to provide resources that can help predict what
> kind of instructional activities will best support stu-
> dents' efforts to achieve learning goals.

> Varying the size of the group for instruction is another
> type of modification that can be used to create an effec-
> tive environment for students with math disabilities.

Regular staff meetings provide an opportunity for school administrators to maintain an ongoing school-wide focus on increased learning for staff and students in mathematics through a continuous process of professional development.

Attending to the emotional, physical and intellectual environment of the mentoring relationship accelerates growth from novice to expert teaching.

This proficiency in the addition, subtraction and multiplication of fractions and mixed numbers should be limited to those with simple denominators that can be visualized concretely and pictorially and are apt to occur in real world settings.

Adaptations and modifications of reinforcement styles or acknowledgment of student progress begin with teachers being aware of different reinforcement patterns.

Keeping a journal begins a lifelong journey of reflective practice.

Sequentially complex tasks can begin to remedy the problem of appropriate challenge in an academically diverse class.

Each of the preceding examples has a similar form. In every example except the third, the subject of the sentence is a long noun construction or an incomplete phrase. In the fourth, fifth and seventh sentences the subject does not match the verb (keeping a journal can't "begin" anything), and in all of them it is hard for the reader to picture the subject performing any kind of action, because the subject is not a person, animal or thing that could take any action. The verb in most of the sentences is followed by an extremely long noun construction; by the time readers find out in the third sentence what regular staff meetings "provide," they have almost forgotten the point of the sentence.

Most of the quotes contain awkward noun-adjectives. In the 1950s Robert Waddell complained that a good deal of English prose had become "a graceless standardized jargon" that relied heavily on noun constructions. According to Waddell,

> The use of noun-adjectives is common in English (stone wall, morning paper, business letter, etc.), but it is usually confined to relatively short nouns, and the relation between noun-adjective and the noun modified is usually clear and simple (time, place, purpose, composition, etc.). But in jargon, the longer the noun-adjective the better; and its relation to the noun modified can be anything—or better yet, everything.

It is not hard to find examples of noun-adjectives in educational writing—"reinforcement patterns"; "school-wide focus"; "learning goals"; "teacher interaction"; "intention-driven questions"; "objectives-driven menu"—or awkward noun constructions—"positive modifications for increasing time for mathematics instruction"; "increased specificity of information"; "instructional connections to student leanings"; "sensemaking activities differentiated by learning modalities"; "instructional variables that are promising for use within a secondary prevention mode."

A good deal of writing in education is, as Waddell said about jargon, "almost nothing but nouns, noun-adjectives, and other noun constructions strung together with relatively meaningless connectives." Such writing often has a monotonous tone and a "shuffling pace and arrhythmic gait." Some educational writers avoid simple, active verbs in favour of multi-syllabic verbs (or verb phrases) derived from Latin that are extremely hard to visualize—"can be related to" (passive constructions are also popular); "provides opportunities for"; "utilizes the potential of" (how exactly do you utilize potential?); "reflects"; "contributes to"; "represents." Students don't just say things—they "verbalize" or "orally respond"—and teachers don't tell students things—they use "verbal prompts." Nouns are often turned into verbs ("no particular learning goals are privileged at the outset") and adjectives are used incorrectly ("effective environment"). The numbing effect of this kind of writing was beautifully described by Orwell: "A mass of Latin words falls upon the facts like soft snow, blurring the outlines and covering up all the details."

Orwell warned about the effects this kind of writing could have:

> A man may take to drink because he feels himself to be a failure, and then fail all the more completely because he drinks. It is rather the same with the English language. It becomes ugly and inaccurate because our thoughts are foolish, but the slovenliness of our language makes it easier to have foolish thoughts . . . Modern English, especially written English, is full of bad habits which spread by imitation and which can be avoided if one is willing to take the necessary trouble. If one gets rid of these habits one can think more clearly . . ."

The style of writing I have described is imitated by students who attend university, and even people who don't enter academia begin to write in a similar style. I have picked up a number of bad habits in the course of my own education: I usually have to rewrite a paragraph several times before the vague, passive and convoluted style that I learned is completely wrung out of each sentence. Orwell gave a clear warning about the effects of sloppy prose in politics, but bad writing also has serious side effects in the social sciences, and in education in particular. Things didn't turn out precisely as Orwell feared they might in the political arena, but he would still undoubtedly be alarmed at the state of the language.

Language is the main tool we have for exploring and

communicating ideas. Prose that is sloppy, vague or inele-
gant is unlikely to guide a writer to new ideas or new discoveries, or, as Orwell pointed out, to prevent the writer
from thinking things that are false or stupid. Clear prose
does not necessarily produce clear thoughts, but it does
allow readers to assess the quality of the writer's ideas and
to understand the implications of those ideas. We have a
robust, vibrant language, and to corrupt it is to do a dis-
service to future generations. This is not simply a matter of
taste. Like any complex system, ordinary language has
evolved to have an expressive power that is beyond anything
a single person could have invented—it can help guide our
thought in a complex world.

There is a growing class of academics who aren't scientists but who are under enormous pressure to produce theories and results that sound like science. Educators should
be rewarded by their departments for writing well, for not
trying to sound learned or scientific by adopting the passive voice or relying too heavily on Latinate verbs and noun
constructions. (I am not implying that scientists are not
good writers. Many are extremely clear, concise and elegant
writers, because they have been trained to think rigorously
and because they have something to say that is supported
by facts.) If educators choose to carry out controlled experiments and to make scientific generalizations, then their
work should meet the highest standards of experimental
rigour. If their goal is more to inspire teachers or convince
them to try certain approaches in the classroom, they
should make an effort to write well.

I have little hope that there will be anything like a rigorous theory of education in our time. To create such a theory we would have to know much more about how the brain works and how to isolate causes and effects in a complex system, whether it be a school or a classroom or even the life of a single child. But we can still make improvements in education, if we are willing to learn from the methods that a new generation of activists and innovators have developed to solve problems in the social sector.

CHAPTER NINE

GENETIC ALGORITHMS IN THE SOCIAL SECTOR

IN 1991 A DOCTOR WORKING AT A HOSPITAL in the slums of Rio de Janeiro, Brazil, noticed that most of the children she treated would end up back in hospital a few days after they were released. Vera Regina Gaensly Cordeiro saw that her efforts to help the children of the slums were largely being wasted, but rather than soldiering on or moving to a more affluent hospital, she decided to try something different. She trained a team of local volunteers and parents to take care of the children properly after they were released. The volunteers learned how to prepare nutritious meals, administer medicine and create sanitary conditions in the children's homes. The rate of re-admittance for the doctor's young patients dropped dramatically.

Although Dr. Cordeiro's new model for caring for slum

children was extremely successful, her ideas were slow to catch on. Social workers who were paid to help the children did everything they could to stop the program from spreading. The doctor had intruded on their domain of expertise; she had no official training in social work and her ideas were different from the ones they had learned in their professional education. It took years of hard work and advocacy by the doctor and her volunteers before the program was accepted in other hospitals in Brazil.

In 1993 Dr. Cordeiro won an Ashoka Fellowship for her work. The Ashoka Fellowships were founded in 1981 by Bill Drayton, who believed that the most effective way to solve social and environmental problems was to fund social activists or "social entrepreneurs" whose innovative solutions could grow to scale, but whose work was still at an early stage. Ashoka has an impressive track record: more than 60 percent of Ashoka fellows, who work in countries around the world, have had an effect on national policy in their field within five years of receiving the fellowship. Two inspiring books, *How to Change the World* and *Getting to Maybe,* give a detailed account of the work of important social entrepreneurs, some of them funded by Ashoka.

Since I received an Ashoka Fellowship in 2003 I have met more than a hundred fellows, but I have never felt that the term "social entrepreneur" completely captures what these people do. *Entrepreneur* comes from the world of business. While business entrepreneurs are often motivated by a desire to improve society or a passion for their product, many have chosen their line of work simply to earn a living.

Entrepreneurs will often change companies for better pay, or retire when they have earned enough money. But all the social entrepreneurs I have met would work for the programs they founded, whether or not anyone paid them, as long as they were able to.

Until recently, business entrepreneurs were deemed successful when either their company or their paycheque had reached a certain size, no matter what kind of product they produced. The company might use misleading advertising to sell cars with low mileage and high emissions, made of toxic, non-recyclable parts, their production subsidized by government grants and tax write-offs—but so long as it outperformed its competitors the entrepreneur would be feted and held up as a role model. While business is finally moving to recognize companies whose products are of real benefit to society and whose production methods are sustainable and environmentally friendly, this trend is unfortunately still marginal.

Social entrepreneurs, by contrast, are not able to separate the social value of their work from the work itself. The most famous social entrepreneur in the world now is probably Muhammad Yunus, who won the 2006 Nobel Peace Prize. In the 1960s Yunus was a professor of economics at a university in Bangladesh. During a famine he decided to set aside the academic theories he had learned as an economist and step out into the streets. He wanted to find out why the international aid that was pouring into his country and his government's efforts to distribute the aid were having so little effect on Bangladesh's crippling poverty. He discovered that the poor couldn't lift themselves out of destitution because they had to take out loans to buy or produce the goods they sold, and the rates charged by loan sharks were so exorbitant that poor working people could never make enough profit to escape the vicious cycle.

Yunus asked the bankers in his country if they would lend small amounts of money to tradespeople and merchants so they would no longer be at the mercy of the loan sharks. The bankers all replied that this was impossible. In their eyes Yunus's request betrayed his ignorance of conventional financial theory: a program that made small loans could never sustain itself because poor people would never repay their loans. Yunus decided to start his own bank, which would make loans as small as a dollar. He soon found that women were more likely to repay the money, as the men would sometimes squander or drink the money away, so he started making loans primarily to women, and he helped them form collectives so that their businesses could grow. The idea of micro-credit, pioneered by Yunus's Grameen Bank, has spread around the world and has helped millions of people escape poverty.

The many social entrepreneurs I have met, through organizations such as Ashoka in the United States and the McConnell Foundation in Canada, have one thing in common with business entrepreneurs: they constantly develop and refine their ideas by trial and error, in much the same way as business people create new products. Social entrepreneurs rarely start with a theory about how a problem might be solved; in fact, they rarely even set out to solve a particular problem. More often a problem is thrust upon them in whatever charitable or professional work they happen to be engaged in, and the solution that emerges over time is usually the result of a great deal of trial and error and many false starts.

The traditional approach to social problems, which was developed largely by academics and bureaucrats, is to create a theoretical solution to a problem and dump it on a system, using the tools of massive investment and directives from the top levels of administration. This is exactly the approach that has been taken in education over the past two decades. In North America, one theory about how children should be taught predominates; it was enshrined in the NCTM standards of the nineties and adopted by school boards and education ministries across the continent. Although there are several textbook companies in North America, there is essentially only one textbook—all the texts used in virtually every school are based on the same theory. David Klein's article "A Brief History of American K–12 Mathematics Education in the 20th Century" contains a revealing account of how educational theorists and government agencies succeeded in making the NCTM standards universal in the United States. A similar history ought to be written for Canada.

Progress in education, and in the social sector as a whole, has been limited because complex problems are rarely solved by imposing general theories on a system from the top down. A theory may work well in some parts of the system or under certain conditions, but if conditions change slightly a whole new set of problems can emerge that the theory is too rigid to respond to. In the 1980s researchers in mathematics and computer science discovered that some extremely complex problems in their fields can be solved more efficiently by an approach called a genetic algorithm, which was inspired by the way strands of DNA combine and are selected by the environment. To solve a problem using a genetic algorithm, a researcher doesn't start with any particular theory about the problem, but instead generates a number of potential solutions, which are usually represented in binary code (the strings of zeros and ones I introduced in chapter four). The researcher then begins to combine the potential solutions by breaking apart the strings of symbols and joining different parts at random. After each round of this process the researcher measures the resulting combinations for fitness (how close a string is to being a good solution) and throws out any combinations that are unfit. A genetic algorithm often solves a complex problem more quickly than any one theoretical approach. Because social problems are so complex, we would be more likely to find robust solutions to them if we were to adopt elements of the genetic algorithm method. The use of trial and error, randomness and constant monitoring and assessment of potential solutions characterize the work of all the social entrepreneurs I have met.

JUMP scarcely bears comparison to such a profoundly important organization as the Grameen Bank, or to the programs started by Ashoka fellows that have had broad national or international effects, but the program developed in much the same way as those programs. JUMP was founded through a series of lucky accidents and grew by trial and error through the work of hundreds of teachers and volunteers. If the program has any value, it lies in features that I could not have foreseen. I would not have believed that abilities could emerge so dramatically in challenged students, or that these students could flourish in regular classes when hierarchies were minimized, or that networks of concerned teachers and administrators could exert such a profound influence on their schools and even their boards of education—unless I had seen those things with my own eyes.

Most social entrepreneurs work in systems that are highly inertial and resistant to change, in which power is centralized and reaches from the top down to the bottom. In such systems, as Dr. Cordeiro discovered, the work of a social entrepreneur will almost certainly intrude on the domain of administrators and bureaucrats. These systems present almost insurmountable barriers to experimentation and use of trial and error, and especially to the introduction of ideas from the outside.

In Canada, ministries of education and school boards employ educational consultants who provide professional development for teachers; they wield a great deal of power in deciding what programs and texts can be used in their province or a board. Over the past three years JUMP has established very productive relations with consultants and staff in many western Canadian school boards and ministries. One western school board has organized and partially funded professional development in JUMP methods for more than eighty teachers, and four teachers have received extensive training as JUMP mentors. The board now even sponsors regular study sessions on JUMP for teachers. In another western province, the education ministry funded a teleconferencing pilot with JUMP, and a second pilot for students who are in trouble with the law. In a third western province a major research pilot is under development, and staff in the ministry of education and in local school boards have formed steering committees that have already overseen several successful pilots.

Some school boards and education ministries in Canada are less centralized and employ fewer educational consultants than others. In those boards teachers are not required to choose materials from a very small set of board-approved textbooks or programs, and they have a good deal of autonomy in their classrooms. But in other boards teachers have started secretly photocopying JUMP materials because the program is not supported by their math consultants. To see how easily new ideas can be supported or thwarted by a school board, it helps to look at several different cases.

The success of JUMP in western school boards is only partly due to the fact that those boards are less centralized and more open to innovation; it also stems from the way the program was introduced. In provinces where JUMP is growing rapidly, I was invited to visit by consultants or by board or ministry staff. In one province a math consultant from a ministry invited me to run an experimental pilot, and in another the provincial association of resource teachers invited me to be a keynote speaker at a professional development conference. Through these initial contacts I quickly met and developed very productive relations with board and ministry staff in the province, and pilots were then set up. The success of the pilots led more teachers, administrators and consultants to advocate for the program.

In the western school board where JUMP has trained more than eighty teachers, a teachers' union representative was primarily responsible for getting the program started in her board. She contacted me while she was visiting Toronto because her colleagues were frustrated with the textbooks their board had purchased. At our first meeting the teacher mentioned that her son had been having trouble with math, so I spent an hour working with him. Later that day she e-mailed me to say that her son was "a different kid," and that he had proudly shown off to his grandparents the work he had done with me. After she tried the JUMP materials with her son and her students, she organized a steering committee of teachers who eventually introduced me to administrators from the school board. A senior consultant for the board gave a seminar on how JUMP methods are supported by new work in cognition, and the board began to hold regular training sessions for teachers.

At a recent study session the teachers shared their ideas about teaching and gave extremely positive reports on the effects of the program in their classes. One teacher brought me a collection of beautiful thank-you letters from her students. Another teacher, who is math-phobic, said she was so inspired by a class she observed that she went home and figured out a formula for the value of terms in a sequence of numbers—and she woke her husband up in the middle of the night to check if it was correct! Another teacher told me she began to be more confident about her own abilities after she had used some of the JUMP materials with her daughter; she wrote the following about the program.

> There is an awareness of emotional intelligence in this program that I love . . . the development of a sense of safety, the stimulation of self worth and value, dignity and a sense of community. It uses techniques of simplification and incremental growth to an exquisite level, but it is the lack of judgment and the presence of honest untainted faith . . . of delicious faith in the capacity of the mind to overcome obstacles in the presence of genuine humanity.

The JUMP program has not received the support in Ontario that it has from boards in western Canada, in spite of an enormous amount of interest from teachers and principals. I believe this is partly because of the way JUMP started. My work for the program is unpaid and I develop materials in my spare time; the organization has only recently had the resources to hire more writers. As a result it has taken about five years to develop JUMP workbooks for the full curriculum.

Consultants who saw our early units—confidence-building exercises emphasizing the need to teach weaker students in extremely small steps—somehow formed the impression that these units were the whole program. The consultants thought that JUMP was a throwback to rote learning and, as such, a threat to all the work they had done. Several extremely influential consultants spoke against JUMP at conferences and informal meetings (well beyond the school boards where they were employed), and word quickly spread among consultants in the province that JUMP was "a threat to education." This very active campaign (carried out by one consultant in particular) brought things to a tipping point among consultants and administrators, accounting, I believe, for the fact that so few boards in Ontario have shown any interest in JUMP, even though it has been welcomed in other provinces and internationally. In at least four boards that I am aware of in Ontario, math consultants have either stopped or discouraged JUMP implementations.

In one school board in Ontario, administrators and teachers at several inner-city high schools tried JUMP with students who were considered at risk of failing or dropping out. The pilots were so successful that they soon spread to some of the elementary feeder schools for these high schools. Teachers and administrators at the schools wanted to extend the pilots, so they approached the math consultant in their board for some of the ministry money that had been allocated for students at risk. School boards are generally thrilled when teachers and administrators from several schools are willing to work together to help kids who are struggling, so the group was optimistic. But the math consultant refused to release any money for the initiative.

When I ran into the consultant at a school where I had been invited to give a talk, I asked her if she would like to know more about JUMP. She told me she had done a good deal of research on JUMP and already knew about the program. I asked her what research she had done, and she replied that she had talked to the math consultants from another city about the program. JUMP had recently produced new books, teacher's manuals and professional development materials that those consultants hadn't seen, so I suggested that looking at the new materials might ease some of her concerns about the program. She replied that she wasn't interested in learning anything more about JUMP. Teachers and administrators who continue to use JUMP materials in that school board—who are having great success with the materials—are reluctant to broadcast this fact for fear of reprisals from the consultant or the administrators who support her. And the consultant continues to publicly air her opinions about JUMP.

In another board, in nine schools that used JUMP with some consistency across an entire grade level, provincial test scores rose fifteen percentage points on average (more than half the schools rose eighteen points or more)—far above the average increase in the province. Rather than showing curiosity about the results, the math consultants in the board tried to discredit them. When I met with them they told me they were convinced that a leap of thirty percentage points in the scores of one school was not due to JUMP, but had occurred because the children in the two classrooms that used JUMP were a very strong cohort.

The consultants had looked up the school's scores from three years back and found that the students had achieved high scores on their Grade 3 province-wide exams. But it turned out they had looked at the wrong set of students. The students in the JUMP classes were in Grade 3, not Grade 6, so they had never written the exams. When the consultants recognized their error, they said that the increase in the scores was likely due to other programs in the school. I told them that the teachers attributed the changes to JUMP, and that JUMP was the only math program they used. Of course, the leap in scores may well have been due to other factors, but if a textbook program had achieved the same results, the consultants would likely have looked into them more deeply, or even allocated money to test the program. Instead of observing JUMP classes or having in-depth conversations with me about the program, they preferred to spend their time looking up old test scores so they could ignore the results.

These are not isolated incidents. My talks have been cancelled by math consultants, a vice-principal once told me he believed he was passed over for promotion because he advocated JUMP, a parent was told by a principal she couldn't talk about JUMP at parents' meetings because of a directive from a superintendent, and teachers who were looking forward to being part of a research pilot in their school were told that the pilot had been cancelled by the consultants. In one affluent school board a senior administrator told a parent that his consultants opposed JUMP and that the board didn't need to consider any new math initiatives because close to 75 percent of the students had scored at grade level or beyond on provincial exams. A teacher in one needy inner-city school once wrote to tell me that in the first year she used JUMP she had brought the provincial scores in her grade up by thirty percentage points, and in the second year only two students in her class failed to score at grade level or beyond. I asked her if she would consider becoming a JUMP mentor, and she told me that she couldn't talk about JUMP because the program had been banned by the consultants in her board. In many school boards a single consultant has almost absolute power over which texts and programs the teachers in the board can use in their classrooms.

It is important to look more closely at why JUMP has met such resistance in some places, because what has occasionally happened to JUMP has happened to countless other initiatives by parents, teachers and administrators in school boards across North America. Some school boards and education ministries have rigid, authoritarian structures that discourage innovation or experimentation and that prevent teachers and principals from taking initiatives to improve their schools. These top-down structures are particularly dangerous when key people in a board or ministry are in conflict of interest.

A year ago I was invited by a provincial ministry to make a presentation on JUMP to a large group of educational consultants from across the province. After my presentation I found out that a group of math consultants in the ministry had written a very negative evaluation of JUMP some weeks before. I was quite upset when I learned that the minds of the people in my audience had probably been made up before I said a word. And I was even more upset when I opened a textbook several weeks later and saw that one of the consultants who had written the evaluation was the senior author of the textbook series. The day I spoke, the textbook company had also been invited to give a presentation. None of the thirty or so consultants who were at my talk has ever contacted me to find out more about JUMP.

Some of the most influential math consultants and educators I have met derive some of their income from textbook companies, even though they are also employed by school boards or education ministries. This conflict of interest would not be tolerated in any other area of public life, and it should not be tolerated in education. It compromises the work of thousands of teachers and administrators. It also prevents school boards and ministries from testing new programs in a scientific spirit, because, as Upton Sinclair once said, "It is difficult to get a man to understand something when his job depends on not understanding it."

A small number of people who receive royalties or salaries from textbook companies can influence a very large number of consultants and administrators who have no connection whatsoever to the publishing side of things. A person who is good at influencing other people can build a network of supporters among people who attend the same conferences or who work in the same school board. As the history of science shows, even highly intelligent and well-educated people like to form tribes, and members of a tribe will stick to their own ways no matter how much evidence you produce that contradicts their beliefs. Even great scientists have sided with the majority when rigorous experimental evidence contradicted the majority view. In education, where so little is known with any degree of certainty and where so much is at stake, the tendency of people to form tribes that exclude people with different opinions and approaches is very dangerous.

Humans are inclined to make instant judgments based on very little knowledge, and we stick to our judgments. In a recent psychological experiment, American Democrats and Republicans were shown tapes of John Kerry and George Bush contradicting themselves. In the researchers' assessments, "Republican subjects were as critical of Kerry as Democratic subjects were of Bush, yet both let their own candidate off the hook." Brain scans of the subjects showed that, while they were watching the tapes, they were processing the information primarily in the emotional part of their brain rather than the rational part.

My advice for any administrator, teacher or parent who has been told by a consultant that JUMP doesn't work is this: ask them how they know JUMP doesn't work. Have they read all the JUMP materials from cover to cover? Have they observed the program for long periods in a variety of classrooms, particularly with lead teachers? Have they talked with people who are experts in the program, or who have had success with the program? Have they read the books and research articles cited in Appendix 1 of this book (including the report "Education For All" published by the Ontario ministry of education) that lend support to the JUMP methods? I would also recommend that people who are concerned about education do research about competing programs with equal care before they make up their minds.

One of the unfortunate ironies in education is that many consultants who advocate discovery-based learning and insist there should be no authority in the classroom are among the most authoritarian people I have met. But they are also, for the most part, among the most dedicated and well-meaning people I have met, and they have worked very hard to improve education. That is why they are willing to fight so hard for the things they believe in. Some of the consultants who have opposed JUMP most strongly work as volunteers helping children in their spare time, just as I do. Understanding this paradox is fundamentally important— people who resist change in any field are often not very different from people who advocate change. We will never make any progress in education until we understand how fallible we all are, how quick we are to make judgments and how susceptible we are to our emotions and to a crowd mentality, whether we are on the side of change or against it. That is why we must work to establish checks and balances in the school system—even against programs like JUMP.

I have not mentioned the names of any school boards in this discussion, not even of boards where JUMP has been welcomed, for two reasons. Administrators in school boards can be very sensitive about the way information is released. I know of one case where a very promising program was cancelled simply because a senior administrator hadn't been told about the program and had learned about it through a newspaper report. This tendency towards defensive territorial behaviour is not peculiar to the education system. There isn't a person alive who isn't prone to this kind of behaviour.

The other reason I have not included any names in this book is because I still have some hope of working with the consultants who have spent so much time trying to ban JUMP. The educational system can become stronger only if it combines different points of view and recognizes the strengths of various approaches.

Several nights ago I attended a parents' council meeting at an inner-city school that was attended by well over a hundred people. A Grade 4 teacher at the school had brought the members of her class to the meeting so I could give a demonstration lesson to the parents on how they could teach mathematics to their kids. During the session the students became very excited about answering questions in front of an audience and the parents got caught up in the excitement. When I invited the parents to take part in the lesson they started putting up their hands with much the same energy as the kids. The head of the parents' council, who is also a JUMP volunteer in the school, proposed that the parents set up study groups to learn how to teach their children and the other parents and the administrators and teachers at the school supported the idea. This is just one example of the enormous reserves of untapped energy that I have observed among parents, teachers and principals that school boards will often thwart when they impose board-wide directives and when they fail to nurture grassroots solutions to problems.

Sometimes the rules established by education ministries and school boards make it very hard for teachers to do their jobs. In Ontario, schools can get ministry funding to buy a textbook only if the book is on the Trillium list. So teachers who use JUMP materials have to find funding from other sources: from temporary innovation funds, from discretionary funds for classroom supplies, and sometimes out of their own pockets (teachers tend to buy many of their supplies out of their own pockets, which most people aren't aware of). Even though our materials are extremely inexpensive, teachers have resorted to photocopying our materials. Based on what I have heard from teachers and parents, I believe that hundreds of classrooms in Ontario are using JUMP materials unofficially. We have sold twenty thousand copies of *JUMP at Home*, and many of those books were bought by teachers or given to teachers by parents who bought them. Many schools have also purchased single copies of the school version of the workbooks from our website. I have donated my work on the JUMP books and I do not lose any money myself when teachers photocopy our materials. But while I am happy that kids are benefiting from the program, the fact that schools can't get funding for JUMP means that we always have trouble meeting our bills as a charitable organization and, thus, reaching more children. And, of course, improvements in classes that are using JUMP materials unofficially are credited to the current teaching practices.

If JUMP were a business and my intention had been to make money, I would have tried to produce a textbook that would be accepted on the Trillium list. Then schools in Ontario could get funding for our material. But I decided not to try to get on the Trillium list because I believe that textbooks, as they are now defined by that list, are not the most cost-effective or efficient means of educating children. To give an example to show why I think this, the Ontario Ministry of Education claims to base its math programs on research. But some of the research they have used is now increasingly being called into question, and isn't supported by new work in cognition. The Trillium list dictates that only books that are durable enough to last for many years can be considered textbooks and receive funding from the ministry. This demand completely contradicts the ministry's claim to be interested in research—a text developed now cannot possibly incorporate all the new findings that will emerge even over the next five years.

But there is an even more serious problem with the way textbooks are produced. Even if there were a teaching model that everyone agreed worked, there would still be an enormous gap between the theoretical model and the actual text. Good materials for kids need to be constantly tested and refined through many iterations. I have written five drafts of some worksheets and I am still improving them, which is why we decided at JUMP to produce workbooks. We may eventually produce textbooks to save on the amount of paper used in the workbooks, but they will be cheap and they will likely be revised more frequently than the books on the Trillium list.

The textbooks used in our schools are based on partly outdated research and are inefficient because they do not allow for revision and improvement—but they are forced to be inefficient by the requirements of the Trillium list. If you look closely at parts of the textbooks used in Ontario, they seem to have been written as much to meet the requirements of the ministry as they were for children. In a Grade 4 book used widely in Ontario, I came across three pages of text describing the steps to use on a computer to get a triangle to appear and how to do some simple manipulations of the shape. Even if I did happen to think this is a good exercise, I wouldn't put it in my text, because very few kids in Grade 4 could read or understand the long explanation. If I wanted kids to do the activity with the computer I would have put it in the teacher's manuals, not the textbook. The material had to be included in the book because the book had to meet the technology requirements for all texts on the Trillium list. It is far more rational to put anything that might be a barrier to kids in a teacher's manual and to include only kid-friendly material in texts or workbooks. But then the books wouldn't get on the Trillium list, because the list mandates that all curriculum requirements must be met in the books themselves. JUMP has opted for a different solution.

Richard Feynman once volunteered to sit on a committee to select math textbooks for the State of California. He tells the story of what happened in his book *"Surely You're Joking, Mr. Feynman!"*. During the selection process Feynman began to suspect that some of the other members of the commission hadn't read the books that were being evaluated very carefully because they kept pressing him for his opinion of the books without telling him theirs. His suspicions were confirmed when a member of the commission asked his opinion of a book that consisted of a set of blank pages bound between a pair of covers. (A textbook company had sent the book hoping it would qualify for evaluation even though the company had missed the deadline). As Feynman says:

> It turned out that the blank book had a rating by some of the other members! They couldn't believe it was a blank, because they had a rating. In fact, the rating for the missing book was a bit higher than for the two others. The fact that there was nothing in the book had nothing to do with the rating . . . It turned out that the other members of the committee had done a lot of work in giving out and collecting the books and had gone to sessions in which the book publishers would explain the books before they read them; I was the only guy on that commission who read all the books and didn't get any information from the book publishers except what was in the books themselves, the things that would ultimately go to the schools.

From what I have observed in several boards, the process by which books are selected for schools has not improved greatly since Feynman's day. Some teachers and principals have told me that they did not have the means to evaluate the books they purchased for their schools properly. Apart from the limited selection of books, they didn't have time to test the books because they had to spend the money allocated for the books before a certain deadline. In some schools, books that the school spent twenty or thirty thousand dollars on are collecting dust on shelves because the teachers do not find them effective.

This is just one of many examples of how things like the Trillium list force inefficiencies on the system and how regulations handed down by a centralized bureaucracy can create problems in the schools. To guard against these inefficiencies there are some things we could do. School boards must be open to running programs that are the educational equivalent of genetic algorithms. Rather than dumping a single theory or textbook on schools wholesale, boards should test a variety of approaches on a smaller scale. They should learn from failure and combine the best of the approaches, while constantly measuring them for fitness.

Throwing money at a problem without establishing rules against conflict of interest and a system of checks and balances won't fix the problem, particularly if boards simply buy more texts of the same type or hire more experts who all believe the same thing and who aren't open to experimentation. When boards hire experts without seeking a range of expertise, they just make it harder for teachers to do their jobs. Boards should establish committees of teachers, parents, administrators and consultants to monitor the success of new programs. People who sit on these committees must have no ties to textbook companies or to anyone who sells materials to schools, nor should they have an intellectual stake in the pilots. Administrators and consultants should be rewarded for their openness to new ideas, including those that come from teachers, and for the rigour with which they evaluate programs—not for being right. School boards must select leaders who are scientists in spirit and who will always remember Alexander Pope's saying, "A little learning is a dangerous thing."

Boards must assume that teachers will be able to tell when their classes improve, will be motivated to improve their teaching, and will have good judgment about the success of their work, if they are offered alternatives that make sense to them and that they can become excited about. Rather than trying to improve schools and by forcing the same text or program on every teacher, boards must trust that teachers who are given a range of resources to test, and who can communicate with their peers about their successes and failures, will become better teachers.

We must move away from a system that values theoretical expertise more than practical expertise. There are teachers who clearly can teach well and who are recognized as good teachers by their colleagues and their students. Find out what these teachers do and allow them to train other teachers. If an educator can't step into either the most difficult inner-city classroom or the most affluent, privileged school and get all of the children engaged, and if they can't give other teachers effective strategies for doing this, then they should not have the power to dictate to teachers.

Kierkegaard once said that Hegel would have been the most profound thinker who ever lived if, when he had finished creating his monumental system of the world, he had simply admitted to himself that it was all only a beautiful thought-experiment. Anyone who works in education and develops theories about how children learn would be wise to keep this comment in mind. I often wonder whether the things I have said about teaching in this book are simply the products of my imagination, and if my delusions have the potential to cause damage in schools. I take some comfort in the fact that teachers would not voluntarily adopt programs even against the wishes of the consultants in their board unless they thought those programs were of some benefit. As long as JUMP is not forced on teachers, it seems to have the potential to add value to their work. I have no idea whether the ideas behind JUMP will turn out to be best practices or whether better methods of teaching will be developed—even within JUMP itself—that are based on completely different ideas. But I know that two things at least cannot be a figment of my imagination: I have seen how quickly teachers, administrators and parents can mobilize to improve their schools if they work in boards that will allow experiments to take place and that will help new approaches grow organically from the bottom up. And I have seen the great potential children have for learning and how much they love to learn. And this is what gives me hope.

CHAPTER TEN

MULTIPLYING POTENTIAL

MY POLITICAL VIEWS are hard to characterize, but I would say I am somewhat left of centre. Lately, though, I've begun to wonder if our debates about which form of government is fairest or most efficient (which, admittedly, have been going on for several thousand years now) are premature. Imagine a group of politicians in ancient Athens, around the time of Plato and Aristotle, arguing about whether they should raise their city's taxes. These male politicians would almost certainly believe that the women of their city were intellectually inferior to the men and that some human beings were by their nature fit only to be slaves, "living tools" who fulfilled their purpose in life by performing duties for higher beings. As Aristotle, one of the enlightened thinkers of his day, said rather chillingly in his Politics,

There must also be an association between that which naturally rules and that which is ruled, with a view to security. That which is able to plan and to take foresight is by nature ruler and master, whereas that which is able to supply physical labor is by nature ruled, a slave to the above. This is why master and slave have a common interest.

From the perspective of this century, the question of whether the citizens of Athens should pay 30 or 40 percent of their income to the government would hardly be the most important issue of the day when two-thirds of Athenians were officially either slaves or other inferior beings who had no right to participate in public life. Now imagine how the politicians of Athens would react if one of their oracles foretold a world in which women were equal to men and slavery was abolished. It would be as if someone had stepped into the cave in which these men had been imprisoned their entire lives and tried to convince them to come out into the sunlight and fresh air. They would not believe that, in the world of their descendants, women and slaves could be born with the ability to plan and take foresight, even if they could imagine this happening.

Now suppose there was a world in which children, almost without exception, were born with a gift for learning anything. And suppose that everyone in the world took this fact for granted. What form of government would the people of this world establish? My imagination fails me here, because I have never lived in a world like the one I describe. For all I know, there could be no government to speak of, because people wouldn't need to be governed. If people were taught to respect and think clearly about the natural world and to value their own capacities and talents, they might well know how to calculate the real cost of the things they bought and produced, and how to assess the damage they would do to themselves and their society by paying more or less than that price—so government agencies wouldn't be needed to regulate their economic behaviour. If they were educated according to their potential, people might need more time than they could find in the day, or even in a lifetime, for all the things they wanted to learn and experience—so time would be their most precious resource. They might work at things that mattered and produce things they could pass on to their descendants, rather than constantly marketing and disposing of almost everything they created—so no one would have to entice them with taxes and incentives to work or produce what they needed.

Perhaps people who understood the concepts of risk and insurance, who understood how much they depended on other members of their society, would protect themselves against the uncertainties of the world by giving some of their money to a governing body. This body might be staffed by experts who enjoyed solving problems with other people and who would approach issues in a spirit of scientific inquiry, knowing that all the other members of the government had been raised with the same opportunities, and were motivated by the same love of public service.

I have never met a person in Canada, or in the various

countries I have visited, who would say that they are living in the best society imaginable. Socialists have always complained that states created by revolutions in the developing world (rather than in the developed world, where Marx predicted communism would appear) aren't really models of socialism, and capitalists have always complained that there never has been unfettered capitalism. People who advocate a blend of socialism and capitalism aren't very happy either. While I am left-leaning, there isn't a place on the political spectrum that looks like paradise to me right now, and I am beginning to wonder if *Right* and *Left* are any more helpful than the various terms we throw around so carelessly in education. When I think about the citizens of the world, about the things they find important or interesting and what they will become excited about or fight for, and when I imagine putting millions of these people together in any form of society, I'm afraid I can't imagine things going much better for humanity than they are at present.

Through my work with children I have come to believe that there is one central question in our time, and that our disillusionment with the forms of government available and our inability to respond effectively to social and environmental crises are connected to this question. The scientific evidence clearly shows that the vast majority of children are born with the ability to learn anything. The evidence also shows that the brain is plastic throughout life and that abilities can be trained or nurtured in brains that have been damaged, so even children who have been neglected in their early life or who happen to have disabilities are probably capable of more than we expect of them. The central question of our time is whether we are willing to act on this evidence.

The political questions that consume so much of our time and evoke so much passion—such as how much of our income we should pay to the government or whether government should be more or less centralized—are only slightly more relevant now than they were in the time of the ancient Greeks, when the majority of people were thought to be inferior beings. The political questions that consume us will never receive an answer that will outlast whatever government happens to be in office. But the question of whether we will educate children according to their potential could be answered, once and for all, in our time.

The investment needed to educate children properly is minimal. It would cost nothing to introduce laws and regulations in our educational system so that textbooks and programs are developed and tested without conflict of interest and with a greater degree of scientific rigour. By changing their style of teaching to take into account new research in cognition, teachers could provide rigorous instruction of the sort that produces experts, while still allowing their students to make discoveries and to play at learning. And by changing the way they think about and assess ability, teachers could abolish artificial hierarchies from their classrooms and allow children to experience the joy of making discoveries and solving problems, both individually and collectively. Rather than spending all of their money on single programs, school boards and education ministries could run genetic algorithms based on examples from the most successful social innovators, and could thereby constantly test and combine the most promising programs. And, as a society, we could simply refuse to settle for programs that do not nurture the potential of all children in every subject. If we were to take these measures immediately, I believe we would see striking improvements in our schools within a matter of years, and in our society within a decade. Since adults can relearn subjects by tutoring or teaching them to children, we could also establish an adult education program that would support the public school system so we could see the benefits from our investment even more quickly. If we were to invest properly in early childhood education, the results would be even more dramatic.

When we try to predict the course of history, we usually draw a line that passes through the present moment, then through a world we can barely see on the horizon and into the unknown. We tend to think that if only we could manufacture more of these products or convince people to take those actions, our situation would steadily improve. But because the world is complex, our efforts to change a particular behaviour or method of production often have much wider, unforeseeable effects, so that history rarely follows the line that we drew. It's hard to say exactly how a society that educated children according to their potential would look. I can imagine there would be less government and fewer regulations, but I can also imagine that there would be more. It is very difficult to speculate about this issue, because a society that educated children according to their potential would produce adults who would be almost unimaginably different from ours.

There is no cure for being human. We are unlikely to become immortal, and we may never agree on any issue of real significance. But there may well be a cure for the worst of the social and environmental problems of our time, and we might even see the effects of this cure within our lifetimes. If we made an effort to educate children according to their potential, they could develop abilities and points of view that would allow them to live in a more equitable and rationally organized society. They might even be happier than us, or, at the very least, more content.

Children need to develop several qualities if they are to realize their full potential as members of society. These qualities, which we could easily nurture in children if we chose to, are a sense of wonder, a sense of risk, a sense of empathy and a sense of hope.

If children couldn't see any beauty in the visible world, we would be concerned about the way they were being educated or brought up. But the majority of students who graduate from our schools are incapable of seeing beauty in the invisible world of natural laws, in the elegant patterns and symmetries of every cell and every star, or in the innumerable connections that extend through space and time and seem to transcend the human intellect and imagination. I was never more spiritual or had a deeper sense of wonder at the universe than I have felt since I started studying mathematics and science. The world now seems to be an endless chain of dizzying vistas and profound mysteries that I would happily explore for the rest of my life.

Many religious thinkers have taught that mathematics is the embodiment of God's most beautiful thoughts. Children would be happier if they were allowed to think those thoughts themselves. Christians sometimes point to the intelligent design of the universe as grounds for believing in the Bible. But the fact that the design of the universe inspires a sense of awe and that even the simplest amoeba is probably beyond our ability to comprehend—and almost certainly beyond our ability to create—doesn't necessarily imply that the laws and tenets of any particular faith are true. However, if children were allowed to develop a sense of mystery or wonder of the kind Einstein wrote about, they would probably also develop a deeper appreciation for the spiritual principles that underlie all faiths. They might also develop a deeper appreciation of the world in which those principles are manifest, and spend more time enjoying and contemplating nature, both physically and intellectually, than in consuming and destroying it so relentlessly.

I will sometimes say to a student who is struggling at school, "Imagine what your life would be like if someone you looked up to—a friend or parent or teacher—had convinced you that the things you love best in life are too boring or too difficult for you to do. What if someone made you dislike your favourite sport—before you had learned to play it well—by forcing you to compete against children who were much older or by always criticizing the way you held your stick or your bat? Your life would be much less interesting and rich than it is now, but you wouldn't even know what you had lost or what was missing. That's what has happened with all the subjects you think are too boring or too difficult for you to learn at school." When they hear this kind of argument children are usually willing to suspend disbelief, and it doesn't take long to convince them that a subject they thought was boring is actually fun. But very few adults will take the risk of learning something again from the beginning, particularly if it's something they struggled with or found boring at school. It is almost impossible for most adults to imagine that a subject like mathematics, for instance, could be beautiful or interesting.

Recently I read a poll that said only 17 percent of adults in Canada are deeply engaged in their jobs. There may be a connection between this rather alarming statistic and the fact that we learned to give up on so many activities and subjects at school. Perhaps we have settled for so little because we are afraid to start anything over again from the beginning. Our imaginations and our horizons have become so limited that we can hardly see the point in trying. Even if we were able to eradicate material poverty in our society, without changing the way children are educated we would still have to deal with our intellectual and spiritual poverty. People would still settle for jobs that touch only the surface of their intellectual and spiritual being and that engage only a fraction of their potential.

There is an undercurrent of competition in our society that starts to pull us towards our employment from the day we enter school, and that diverts us from the real purpose of our education. If people visit a park to watch a sunset, does it matter who walked there fastest or climbed the highest hill? These achievements may be noteworthy or admirable, but they are not really the point of visiting the park. If children were encouraged to learn things for their own sake— for the beauty of the ideas and the joy of making discoveries and seeing connections—rather than to get the best mark or be better than their peers, they might be less inclined when they are adults to compete for positions and possessions that mean so little to them.

With a sense of wonder comes a sense of humility. Newton once said that he had seen farther by standing on the shoulders of giants. When he compared himself to a schoolboy playing with pebbles on the shore, he showed an even deeper humility. Even though he had discovered the most fundamental laws of the universe, he felt he had only examined a few pebbles washed up by the waves. Many of us have never felt this sense of humility, because we have never understood the immensity of the sea.

To live in harmony with the world, it is not enough for a society to possess a love of nature. If you watch TV for more than fifteen minutes, you will almost certainly see a car or SUV driving through a stretch of beautiful, untouched wilderness. When car companies first invented these ads they clearly hoped that people who watched the ads would flock to the wild, driving greater distances to get to more and more remote places. The car companies took a risk, of course, because there was always a chance people would realize that the pollution the cars created and the roads and industries they brought with them were a threat to the places shown in the ads. But the gamble paid off; no one got upset or complained about the blatant contradiction between the beautiful landscapes and the cars that went racing and skidding through them—because no one could actually see the contradiction. And the ads clearly worked: people now drive more often, for greater distances and in larger vehicles than they ever have.

Our generation lacks any real understanding of cause and effect, of the relative size of effects and how quickly small effects can accumulate. In spite of the billions we have spent on education we have created a society that has very little sense of risk. That is why we face so many crises now, and why we are probably in deeper trouble than we recognize. The majority of people on earth aren't even functionally literate or numerate. If educated people are so easily misled by politicians and advertisers, and have so little ability to assess the consequences of their actions, what will happen when the rest of the world start to demand, as they are beginning to do, that they be able to live like us?

To see the extent to which well-educated people lack a realistic sense of risk, you just have to look at the way they take care of their families. Well-educated parents will drive across town in an SUV to pick up a toy for their children, intending to do something wonderful for them, without any sense of the true cost of the toy or of how their children will pay that cost in twenty years. And their generosity will often stop at their front door. Many parents will spend a large proportion of their income on their children but give only a tiny fraction to charity. There is no better way to put your own children at risk than to ignore the children outside the door—unless, of course, you want your children never to leave the house.

Few people seem to understand that even if a threat is not certain to materialize, it can still be a risk. For fifteen years politicians refused to take any action on global warming because a handful of scientists (mostly on the payroll of the oil companies) claimed that global warming either didn't exist or wasn't due to our actions. But the fact that the overwhelming majority of scientists disagreed with the skeptics meant that the odds that global warming was occurring were extremely high. If you bought a car whose brakes were as likely to fail as our carbon emissions are to cause devastation, you would almost certainly be killed.

The great advantage of capitalism is that people will pay for things that have value. The great disadvantage is that they will also pay for things that are worthless. Capitalism can't work if people don't have the necessary logical or conceptual abilities or understanding of the natural world to calculate the real cost or value of the goods they produce or the risks involved in producing those goods. The idea that the free market will establish a fair or rational price for the things that free agents wish to buy and sell—regardless of how selfish or stupid the people who are buying and selling happen to be—is clearly nonsense.

Even if people have a clear understanding of risk, they may still do next to nothing to protect society against a potential threat if they think there is a good chance they and their children will escape unharmed. A society can flourish only if its citizens have a sense of empathy or charity that extends beyond their immediate families. I have had a fortunate life, and so has my family. The vast majority of people in the world have not. I cannot escape the feeling that this is extremely unfair; I have trouble separating my family from the other families of the world.

A sense of empathy or charity has to be learned. I acquired the conviction that I should help other people from my parents. When I was growing up my parents would billet students from Africa so they could go to our local university. My father often worked for free as a surgeon in African hospitals, and my mother helped administer and raise funds for several Third World charities (she was recognized by the federal government for her work). I started JUMP because I felt I wasn't living up to their example.

If children don't learn empathy from their parents, they must learn it from their teachers. But very few children who are struggling at school feel a deep sense of empathy or connection with their teachers. No matter how loving the teachers are, they still have to withhold the praise and success a child thrives on. That is why we must give teachers the training and materials they need to help every student be successful, and why we should do everything we can to eliminate artificial hierarchies from the classroom. Children will be more inclined to develop a sense of empathy for other people if they are not being constantly ranked and compared to their classmates in what seems to be an arbitrary way.

Even if people have a sense of wonder, a sense of risk and a sense of empathy, they will not act without a sense of hope. When rats are repeatedly exposed to unavoidable shocks or stresses, they develop a learned helplessness and stop trying to escape from their cage, even if they are presented with a way out. A similar sense of helplessness may be the least visible but deepest effect of our schooling. Children are born with a confidence that encourages them to try things that should be impossible—such as walking or learning to talk—and with a sense of wonder that inspires them to look behind every curtain and open every door. But in the course of their education, one door after another is closed, and every year there is one more thing they can't do well or that doesn't interest them. Eventually they learn a sense of helplessness so deep that as adults they will talk about their likes and dislikes, their abilities and disabilities, as though they were expressions of their true nature or genetic makeup, or even of their soul, rather than the product of their experiences.

I have often wondered if the helplessness we feel in the face of environmental and social crises is related to the helplessness we must often have felt as children, when we saw that no matter how hard we tried we would never succeed in doing or understanding something our teachers thought was important. I know many people who are deeply concerned about the kind of world they will pass on to their children, but who can't seem to stop shopping and driving and eating as if the resources of the earth, including its very atmosphere, were inexhaustible—perhaps because they learned at some point when they were young (so long ago now they can't remember when this particular lesson occurred) that they will never be the ones to understand anything too deeply, or excel at anything, or save the situation. And there is no point calling on their friends for help, because their friends don't understand anything either, and because no one could ever get excited about solving a problem together.

Several weeks ago I walked into a Grade 4 class in an inner-city school and was surprised to see a body lying on the floor with a coat draped over its head. This student (a boy as it turned out) apparently came to school most mornings in a depressed and listless state. His teacher suspected that something at home had upset him. I told the boy that I was going to teach a very interesting lesson on fractions, and I asked him to please go back to his desk so I could get started. The boy just stared at me blankly, and neither the teacher nor his best friend could persuade him to stand up. It was clear that I would have to start the lesson with the boy lying at my feet, so I told him he could stay where he was if he was comfortable. I also bent down and showed him how to add on his fingers in case he wanted to take part in the lesson. I showed his classmates how to add a pair of fractions with the same denominator, and a few minutes later, when the children were waving their hands to answer a question, the boy suddenly put up his hand and answered the question while he was still lying on the floor. I found it quite comical to see his hand shoot up from the floor every time I asked a question, but the other children didn't seem to see anything odd in this. After I had given the boy a chance to show off with several questions, he stood up and went back to his desk. He finished all the work that the other children did, and even asked for extra questions when the lesson was over.

Children do have the capacity to pick themselves off the floor—if they can see a point in standing up. For many years they will believe, in spite of evidence to the contrary, that they are capable of doing whatever they set their minds to and that it is worth trying something again and again. But they will not keep trying forever. Some people can't remember having a sense of optimism about school after they reached a certain age. They can remember only a long adjustment to the world of adults, to which they were guided by their grades and by interminable rows of Xs on their papers.

Children will never fulfill their extraordinary potential until we remember how it felt to have so much potential ourselves. It will take some effort to remember who we were before our personalities and our beliefs were formed, when hope was the most common thing in the world, and even the simplest things were possible. There was nothing we weren't inspired to look at or hold, or that we weren't determined to find out or do, like opening a door that could lead to a different world—even if it was only the entrance to a playground or a school—so a child could pass through.

RESEARCH THAT SUPPORTS JUMP METHODS

Many papers and books in psychology and education contain results that lend support to the teaching methods used in JUMP Math. Several of the most rigorously argued and best written of the texts that I have read are listed below. I was helped in making this selection by Dr. Melanie Tate from the Ontario Institute for Studies in Education at the University of Toronto (OISE/UT).

In chapter eight of this book I argued that research in education or in psychology should not be taken as the gospel truth. I cite the research mainly to show that, contrary to the claims of some educators, there is a large body of formal research in education and in psychology that supports the methods used in JUMP. There is clearly enough evidence, both in the literature on education and in informal studies of JUMP (such as the Lambeth report and the scores of testimonials from teachers that are posted on our website), to suggest that school boards should take a closer look at the program. There is only one way a board can determine whether JUMP has any value or not: teachers who wish to try the program, and who are adequately trained in the JUMP methods, should be allowed to run pilots using our materials and the results of these pilots should be evaluated by impartial committees made up of various stakeholders in the schools' boards (and not only by math consultants).

Many educators claim that "discovery-based" and constructivist programs are well supported by the results of cognitive science. The NCTM standards which govern curriculum development in the U.S. and in Canada are based in large part on constructivist research. But many cognitive scientists and educators have recently written papers that take issue with this claim. The paper "Applications and Misapplications of Cognitive Psychology to Mathematics Education" should be required reading for educators and math consultants. It is written by three of the most distinguished cognitive scientists in the world, John Anderson, Lynn Reder and Herb Simon, and they argue that educational movements like constructivism have "questionable psychological foundations." Drawing on their own work, and on numerous studies in cognition, the authors challenge the central claims of the constructivist school, for example: that training by abstraction is of little use, that real learning occurs in authentic situations, that construction needs to be done in a highly social environment, that knowledge cannot be instructed by a teacher but rather it can only be constructed by the learner, that knowledge cannot be represented symbolically and that knowledge can only be communicated in complex learning situations. To the claim that knowledge can always be communicated best in complex learning situations, the authors provide the contrary evidence that "a learner who is having difficulty with components can easily be overwhelmed by the processing demands of a complex task. Further, to the extent that many components are well mastered, the student wastes much less time repeating these mastered operations to get an opportunity to practice the few components that need additional effort." And in response to the NCTM's rejection of the view that "mathematics consists of an accumulation of mathematical concepts and skills," the scientists write "We can only say we find frightening the prospect of mathematics education based on such a misconceived rejection of componential analysis."

In "Why Minimal Guidance During Instruction Does Not Work: An Analysis of the Failure of Constructivist, Discovery, Problem-Based, Experiential and Inquiry-Based Teaching" Paul Kirschner, John Sweller and Richard Clark argue

> After a half century of advocacy associated with instruction using minimal guidance, it appears that there is no body of research supporting the technique. In so far as there is any evidence from controlled studies, it almost uniformly supports direct, strong instructional guidance rather than constructivist-based minimal guidance during the instruction

of novice to intermediate learners. Even for students with considerable prior knowledge, strong guidance while learning is most often found to be equally effective as unguided approaches. Not only is unguided instruction normally less effective; there is also evidence that it may have negative results when students acquire misconceptions or incomplete or disorganized knowledge.

The authors present several reasons why, based on the architecture of the brain, instruction with minimal guidance is not likely to be effective. They argue, for instance, that unguided instruction does not take account of the limitations of a student's working memory: the mind can only retain so much of new information or so many component steps at one time.

In *The Neuropsychology of Mathematics: Diagnosis and Intervention* Steven Feifer and Philip De Fina argue that "teaching students proper decision making skills and algorithmic procedures can profoundly influence mathematics achievement." And furthermore, that "low achieving elementary school students exposed to systematic training in problem solving, decision making skills, and self-monitoring techniques consistently outperformed a control group when solving math word problems. Clearly, specific training on strategy formation skills when engaged in any academic endeavor will free up working memory systems bogged down by inefficient learning styles." Feifer's book also makes the case that students' minds work more effectively when students are less anxious. In "The Use of Scaffolds for Teaching Higher-Level Cognitive Strategies" Barak Rosenshine and Carla Meister argue that teachers should provide scaffolding (hints, reminders and necessary background knowledge and skills) to teach problem solving and higher-order thinking skills effectively. In "The Expert Mind," which I discussed in this book, Philip Ross argues that studies in cognition show that expert abilities can be fostered in children through practice and rigorous instruction.

In "Mindful of Symbols" cognitive scientist Judy DeLoache argues that "less may be more when it comes to educational books for young children." DeLoache found that the more cluttered and distracting the pages of a reader are, the less children learn from the book. DeLoache also tells a success story:

> Using blocks designed to help teach math to young children, we taught six- and seven-year-olds to do subtraction problems that require borrowing (a form of problem that often give young children difficulty). We taught a comparison group to do the same but using pencil and paper. Both groups learned to solve the problems equally well—but the group using the block took three times as long to do so. A girl who used the blocks offered us some advice after the study: "Have you ever thought of teaching kids to do these with pencil and paper? It's a lot easier."

In "Inside the Black Box: Raising Standards Through Classroom Assessment" educators Paul Black and Dylan Wiliam argue that rather than simply assigning students tests at the ends of units, teachers should use continuous assessment (assigning smaller tests and assignments more frequently and giving students immediate feedback) and formative assessment (using the information gathered from tests and assignments to adapt instruction to meet students' needs) to raise standards. Wiliam has said in public talks that if teachers worry less about covering the curriculum, and start by assessing what their students actually know and work from there, they will ultimately cover far more curriculum. (I have seen an enormous amount of evidence for this claim in JUMP.)

Thomas Guskey asserts in "How Classroom Assessments Improve Learning" that "teachers who develop useful assessments, provide corrective instruction and give students second chances to demonstrate success can improve their instruction and help students learn." In "Assessment, Student Confidence and School Success" Richard Stiggins argues that teachers should use assessment to motivate and build confidence rather than to punish or rank students, and in "Students Need Challenge, Not Easy Success" Margaret Clifford makes the case that students benefit when they are given prompt, specific feedback on their work and when they are allowed to take "moderate risks." In JUMP these risks are provided when teachers constantly raise the bar and challenge students to take more and more steps by themselves. JUMP workbooks are designed to allow for continuous formative assessment—the books show teachers how to break material into steps and assess component skills and concepts in every area of the curriculum.

In *Breakthrough,* Michael Fullan, Peter Hill and Carmel Crévola argue that teachers must be trained to use formative assessment and to give instruction that "is sufficiently precise and focused to build directly on what students already know and to take them to the next level." They present a very interesting proposal for allowing boards to develop "expert systems" for developing and implementing solutions to problems, and recommend that boards nurture the growth of communities of educators who can learn from each other.

Many studies have shown that students do better when they are less anxious (for instance Tobias, 1978) and when teachers are consistently supportive and encouraging about students' abilities (Turner, Meyer, Midgely and Patrick, 2003). Kenneth Ruthven has written on the dangers of stereotyping students according to ability and James Hiebert, Anne Morris and Brad Glass argue that teachers "should be inclined and be able to treat the lessons they teach as experiments," so they can constantly refine and improve their techniques. In *Finding Our Way* Margaret Wheatley argues that top down approaches to complex problems often fail in school systems. "A Brief History of American K–12 Mathematics Education in the 20th Century" by David Klein gives a very informative overview of the history of the math wars in the United States.

In 2005 the Ontario Ministry of Education published "Education for All," a report about literacy and numeracy instruction for students with special education needs. It advocates that schools adopt a "Universal Design for Learning," a method for redesigning curriculum and text materials for greater accessibility for all students, which is based on the premise that each student can benefit from a flexible curriculum offering clear goals, multiple pathways to success and fair and accurate assessment. I believe that JUMP has the features of a such a Universal Design for Learning.

As the report recommends, JUMP provides differentiated instruction though a balance of shared, guided and independent learning strategies and tools. These allow teachers to display a positive and encouraging attitude; use simple and clear instructional language; use scaffolding and guided practice; have a means of diagnosing students' prior knowledge and their own prior knowledge; practise frequent and accurate ongoing assessment; show correlations with everyday life; teach the modelling of problems; and help students understand the "big ideas." The JUMP materials also meet the criteria for a scaffolded lesson as identified in the report because they enable teachers to engage in pre-planning; establish a clear goals in lessons; identify student needs and monitor progress by assessing current knowledge and barriers to progress; provide tailored assistance (with a range of supports from remedial to enriched); maintain pursuit of the goal through questioning, praise and encouragement; control for frustration and risk by incrementally raising the level of difficulty; and assist internalization, independence and generalization through a balance of guided practice, problem solving and conceptual extensions.

The "Education For All" report asserts that "outcomes for children across ability levels and for children with specific difficulties in mathematics are improved when math problem solving instruction is overt, systematic and clear and scaffolded by the teacher and peers." It also concludes that "in general, whole class instruction in mathematics has been shown to be effective when both procedural skill and conceptual knowledge are explicitly targeted for instruction: this type of instruction improves outcomes for children across ability levels and grades." The methods of JUMP are strongly supported by the conclusions of the Ministry's report.

MORE INFORMATION ABOUT JUMP MATH

WHAT IS JUMP MATH?

JUMP Math is a philosophy and a set of materials and methods that aims to improve the teaching of mathematics and to help students enjoy and meet their potential in the subject.

The JUMP program is based on the belief that all children in the regular school system, even those diagnosed as having serious learning disabilities, or who are failing, can do well at math. Mathematics, rather than being the most difficult subject, is one in which children can most easily succeed, even at a young age, and can thereby develop the confidence and cognitive abilities they need to do well in other subjects.

The JUMP Math philosophy is based on several important beliefs:

- New intellectual abilities can emerge suddenly in even the most challenged student from a series of small advances, just as a chemical solution can suddenly change colour entirely with the addition of a single drop of reagent. More than any other subject, math is a tool for adding, in a methodical and effective way, the drops of knowledge that will transform a student.

- This non-linear potential can only be nurtured if students are confident and attentive. Teachers must pay attention to the psychology of the classroom to make sure that everyone is included, involved and participating and supported with responsive instruction, praise and encouragement. Children who don't believe they can succeed will never do so. The JUMP program starts with a confidence-building exercise that has demonstrably changed children's perceptions of their abilities.

- By adopting the methods and principles of JUMP Math, schools can teach mathematics to a higher standard, without leaving students behind, and in a cost-effective manner. There will always be differences among students, but we don't need to exaggerate or highlight them by setting up unnecessary hierarchies. By using materials and methods that minimize differences, teachers can cover more of the curriculum and can narrow or close the wide gap in student performance that exists in most classrooms.

• Teachers will only succeed in helping all levels of students when they know how to determine what the students know, how to reduce concepts into the most basic elements of perception and understanding and how to extend ideas in a way that is both engaging and which takes into account the students' readiness to move forward.

WHAT IS JUMP MATH'S APPROACH?

• The JUMP Math program provides teachers with an effective and balanced set of lessons and assignments for students. The work is both concrete and symbolic, both guided and independent and both procedural and conceptual.
• JUMP materials and professional development show teachers how to break mathematical concepts into the most fundamental units of perception and understanding, how to assess and fill in gaps in students' knowledge, how to design sequential, scaffolded lessons, how to understand and present mathematical ideas in different styles and from different perspectives, how to motivate weaker students and how to foster problem solving abilities through graduated challenges and open-ended explorations.
• Teachers cope with large, diverse classes and serious time constraints, and they are often not comfortable

with their own abilities to teach mathematics. Because we know this, JUMP materials cover the curriculum from Grades 1 to 8 completely, substantially reducing the time and cost of photocopying and pulling together materials from various sources. Teachers are encouraged to use the time saved to work on extending their own knowledge of mathematics, enhancing their teaching strategies and improving their planning. The JUMP materials and professional development are designed to help teachers become better math teachers.

- In a typical JUMP lesson, teachers work with the whole class to lead students through a process of guided discovery while also adapting the lessons to each student's level of understanding. Whole-class lessons allow students to experience the thrill of discovery together, as a collective.

- JUMP materials and professional development enable teachers to identify students' needs and monitor their progress by assessing current levels of knowledge and barriers to progress. The materials also allow teachers to provide tailored assistance with a full range of supports.

- Students are guided through steps they can manage, beginning with simple models of the problem. This method of "guided discovery" is very different from rote learning in that students are expected to take the steps themselves. With growing confidence and focus from constant success, students become ready to work more independently and discover more complex mathematical principles on their own.

- Children do better when teachers communicate the belief that all students can learn, and, whenever possible, reinforce the belief with frequent and specific encouragement. Praise and encouragement are integral parts of JUMP Math's approach.
- JUMP workbooks provide review exercises that go back several grade levels for students who have forgotten material or who didn't learn it properly in the first place.
- Workbooks and support materials are designed to allow for continuous assessment by enabling teachers to see exactly where students have understood or failed to understand concepts and operations. But teachers should not expect students to use the workbooks without instruction. Suggestions on how to build dynamic lessons around the workbooks are contained in this book and in the JUMP teachers' manuals and professional development material.

WHAT MATERIALS DOES JUMP MATH PRODUCE?

JUMP Math has developed workbooks for the standard curriculum for Grades 1 to 8 (workbooks for Grades 1 and 2 will be available in September 2007). Each workbook comes in two parts and the strands of the curriculum are revisited twice, once in the first book and again in the second book. The workbooks come with a teachers' manual, which contains mental math exercises, activities and enriched questions that go with the worksheets, as well as suggestions on how to teach the material. In September 2007 JUMP Math will release revised workbooks for Grades 3 to 6 with new teachers' manuals that contain lesson plans for all worksheets.

Two new books are in preparation and will be released during the 2007/2008 academic year, *A Guide to Problem Solving in Mathematics* and *Understanding and Remembering Number Facts*. Also coming in 2007/2008 is a series called "Enriched Lessons in Mathematics for Every Student." The first titles in this series will be *Mathematics and Magic Tricks, Mathematics and Art, Mathematics and Nature, Mathematics and Sports* and *Mathematics and Secret Codes*.

Significant discounts for bulk orders are available to educators. John Mighton has donated his work on the JUMP books and all proceeds from the sale of JUMP books go to JUMP Math. Information on how to order JUMP materials and which materials are currently available is on the JUMP Math website at www.jumpmath.org.

HOW CAN I WORK WITH JUMP MATH?

TEACHERS

Teachers across Canada have formed steering committees and study groups to implement the program and to help JUMP Math build connections with administrators and consultants in school boards. Some teachers have trained to become JUMP mentors who can provide information and professional development to other teachers. JUMP Math offers professional development sessions for teachers by request. By September 2007 online training will be available on our website.

ADMINISTRATORS

JUMP has formed very productive relationships with many schools and school boards. Several pilots in Canada and Britain have shown that, with the support of administrators, JUMP can mobilize and inspire teachers to improve their teaching. We welcome the opportunity to implement pilots in any school or school board that would like to test the program.

PARENTS

JUMP is working with parents' councils and groups to improve the teaching of mathematics in their schools and also to help parents tutor and give academic support to their children.

EDUCATORS AND EDUCATIONAL CONSULTANTS

JUMP welcomes to the opportunity to work with educators to test and refine the methods used in the program. Several formal research studies of JUMP are currently being developed by professors of education and clinical psychologists.

VOLUNTEERS

JUMP trains and places volunteer tutors in the Toronto District School Board and has also helped volunteers establish tutoring clubs in many other locations in Canada and overseas.

DONORS

JUMP Math is a registered not-for-profit organization and a charity. Most of our funding comes from foundations, corporations and individual donors. Donations are used to develop and test materials, to train teachers, parents and tutors, to set up JUMP volunteer tutoring clubs and chapters, to develop partnerships with schools and school boards and to establish book funds that allow us to give materials at a discount or for free to needy schools. You can donate online at www.jumpmath.org or by sending a cheque made out to JUMP Math to 349–401 Richmond Street West, Toronto, Ontario, M5V 3A8.

SOURCE NOTES

CHAPTER ONE: THE WASTE ETHIC

p. 3 "The most beautiful and deepest . . .," White and Gribbin.

CHAPTER TWO: THE EMERGENT MIND

p. 26 "People used to think . . .," Szyf quoted in Waters, p. 34

p. 26 "The impact of experience on cognitive ability . . .," U.S. Department of Education.

pp. 27–28 "A mere twenty years ago . . .," Schwartz and Begley, p. 366

p. 28 "Whatever function a patient . . .," Schwartz and Begley, p.191

CHAPTER THREE: MISTAKING THE ENDS FOR THE MEANS IN EDUCATION

p. 44 "The preponderance of psychological evidence . . .," Ross.

p. 45 "it is possible for enthusiasts . . .," Ross.

p. 61 "only constructed knowledge . . .," Hirsch.

p. 62 "into the roll of passive receptacles . . .," Phillips, pp. 5–12

p. 64 "set the following expectations . . .," Burns.

p. 68 "success comes from understanding . . .," Burns.

p. 70 "mathematics and science are learned . . .," NCTM standards quoted in Klein.

CHAPTER FOUR: PAYING ATTENTION TO ATTENTION

pp. 86–88 "the response to the JUMP pilot . . .," Aduba.

p. 88 "the simple act of paying attention . . .," Schwartz and Begley, p. 18

p. 89 "Our brains allocate space . . .," Schwartz and Begley, p. 224

pp. 96–97 how intelligence evolved in humans, Greenspan and Shanker, pp. 182–83

p. 100 testing children's television programs, Gladwell, pp. 99–132

p. 114 "discriminate among vibrational . . .," Schwartz and Begley, pp. 210–11

CHAPTER FIVE: THE TRIBE THAT COULDN'T COUNT

pp. 118–19 Piaget's experiment and subsequent research, Dehaene.

pp. 119–20 Piaget's experiment on object permanence, Talbot.

p. 120 Piaget's ideas on developmental phases, Dehaene.

p. 122 "the lack of number words . . .," Gordon quoted in Dingfeldere, p. 30

p. 123 "when infants learn to speak . . .," Borovik, pp. 17–43

p. 126 "I find it quite amazing . . .," Feynman, 1967, pp. 170–71

p. 136 "Funes the Memorious," Borges, Irby and Yates, pp. 59–67

CHAPTER SIX: ANT HILLS AND HOLOGRAMS

p. 160 paying attention to the definitions of words, Wittgenstein, p. 103

p. 163 "Education seems to be plagued . . .," Wu, pp. 1–7

p. 164 "Algorithms not only are not . . .," Kamii and Dominick, pp. 130–40

p. 165 "proponents of basic skills . . .," Klein.

p. 171 "the addition algorithm . . .," Wu, pp. 1–7

CHAPTER SEVEN: COLLECTIVE INTELLIGENCE

p. 191 Durkheim's "collective effervescence," Durkheim, p. 134

CHAPTER EIGHT: WORDS FALLING LIKE SNOW: ORWELL'S WARNING

p. 216 paradigm shifts, Kuhn.

pp. 218–20 "The classes that followed . . .," Wilf, pp. 4–5

p. 221 "Performace in many of the indicators . . .," Klein.

p. 222 "in the existing research . . .," Leinwand and Fleishman, pp. 88–89

p. 222 "the Pesek and Kirshner study . . .," Brown, Seidelmann and Zimmermann.

p. 223 "achieved no more and probably less . . . ," Pesek and Kirshner, pp. 524–40

p. 225 "From a total of 8,727 . . .," Klein.

pp. 229–30 "I returned and saw under the sun . . .," Orwell quoted in Wermuth, pp. 98–109

p. 232 "The use of noun-adjectives . . .," Waddell quoted in Wermuth, pp. 84–98

CHAPTER NINE: GENETIC ALGORITHMS IN THE SOCIAL SECTOR

p. 237–38 The work of Dr. Cordeiro, Bornstein.

p. 252 "Republican subjects were as critical . . .," Shermer, p. 36

p. 258 "It turned out that the blank book . . .," Feynman, 1997, pp. 288–303

CHAPTER TEN: MULTIPLYING POTENTIAL

p. 263 "There must also be an association . . .," Aristotle, p. 383

p. 270 poll about engagement at work, Galt.

APPENDIX I: RESEARCH THAT SUPPORTS JUMP METHODS

p. 279 Lambeth report, Aduba.

p. 280 "a learner who is having difficulty . . .," Anderson, Reder and Simon.

pp. 281–82 "After a half century of advocacy . . .," Kirschner, Sweller and Clark, pp. 75–86

p. 282 "teaching students proper decision making . . .," Feifer and De Fina, pp. 65–66

p. 283 scaffolding technique, Rosenshine and Meister, pp. 26–33

p. 283 "less may be more when . . .," DeLoache.

pp. 283–84 continuous assessment, Black and Wiliam, pp. 139–44

p. 284 "teachers who develop useful assessments . . .," Guskey, p. 7

p. 284 using assessment to motivate students, Stiggins.

p. 284 giving students feedback, Clifford, pp. 22–26

p. 285 "is sufficiently precise . . .," Fullan, Hill and Crévola, p. 52

p. 285 students' performance when they are less anxious, Tobias.

p. 285 teachers being consistently supportive, Turner, Meyer, Midgely and Patrick, pp. 1521–58

p. 285 the dangers of stereotyping, Ruthven, pp. 243–53

p. 285 "should be inclined and be able to treat . . .," Hiebert, Morris and Glass, pp. 201–22

p. 285 why top-down approaches fail, Wheatley, pp. 101–13

p. 285 history of math education in the United States, Klein.

pp. 285–87 report recommending a Universal Design for Learning, Ontario Ministry of Education.

BIBLIOGRAPHY

Aduba, Nikai, "JUMP Mathematics Pilot Evaluation—Lambeth." *JUMP Math*, http://jumpmath.org/research/research=initiatives (accessed March 7, 2007).

Anderson, John R., Reder, Lynne M. and Simon, Herbert A., "Applications and Misapplications of Cognitive Psychology to Mathematics Education." *Texas Educational Review* (Summer 2000).

Aristotle and Bambrough, R., *The Philosophy of Aristotle*. Translated by A.E. Wardman and J.L. Creed. New York: New American Library, 1963.

Black, Paul and Wiliam, Dylan, "Inside the Black Box: Raising Standards Through Classroom Assessment." *Phi Delta Kappa* (October 1998).

Bodanis, David, *E Equals Mc²*. New York: Walker & Company, 2005.

Borges, J.L., Irby, J.E. and Yates, D.A., *Labyrinths*. New York: New Directions Publishing Corp., 1962.

Bornstein, David, *How To Change the World*. New York: Oxford University Press, 2004.

Borovik, Alexandre, "Coxeter Theory: The Cognitive Aspects." *The Coxeter Legacy: Reflections and Projections*, Toronto: Fields Institute Communications. no. 46 2006.

Brown, Susan, Seidelmann, Antoinette and Zimmermann, Gwendolyn, "In the Trenches: Three Teachers' Perspectives on Moving Beyond the Math Wars." *Mathematically Sane*, http://mathematicallysane.com/analysis/trenches.asp (accessed March 7, 2007).

Burns, Marilyn, "10 Big Math Ideas." *Instructor Magazine*, (March 2005).

Childress, Stacey, Elmore, Richard and Grossman, Allen, "How to Manage Urban School Districts." *Harvard Business Review* (November 2006).

Clifford, Margaret M., "Students Need Challenge, Not Easy Success." *Educational Leadership* (September 1990).

Dehaene, Stanislas, *The Number Sense: How the Mind Creates Mathematics*. New York: Oxford University Press, 1997.

DeLoache, Judy S., "Mindful of Symbols." *Scientific American* (August 2005).

Dingfeldere, Sadie F., "Fuzzy Math." *Monitor on Psychology*, (February 2005).

Durkheim, Emile, *The Elementary Forms of Religious Life*. New York: Free Press, 1965.

Feifer, Steven G. and De Fina, Philip A., *The Neuropsychology of Mathematics: Diagnosis and Intervention*. Riverside, CA: RET Center, 2005.

Feynman, Richard, *The Character of Physical Law*. Cambridge, MA: MIT Press, 1967.

Feynman, Richard, *"Surely You're Joking, Mr. Feynman!"*. New York: W.W. Norton & Company, 1997.

Fullan, Michael, Hill, Peter and Crévola, Carmel, *Breakthrough*. Thousand Oaks, CA: Corwin Press / Ontario Principals Council / National Staff Development Council, 2006.

Galt, Virginia, "Fewer workers willing to put in 110%," *The Globe and Mail*, Thursday, November 15, 2005.

Gladwell, Malcolm, *The Tipping Point*. London: Little Brown and Company, 2000.

Greenspan, Stanley and Shanker, Stuart, *The First Idea: How Symbols, Language, and Intelligence Evolved from our Primate Ancestors to Modern Humans*. Cambridge, MA: Da Capo Press, 2004.

Guskey, Thomas, "How Classroom Assessments Improve Learning." *Educational Leadership* (February 2003).

Hiebert, James, Morris, Anne K. and Glass, Brad, "Learning to Learn to Teach: An 'Experiment' Model for Teaching and Teacher

Preparation in Mathematics." *Journal of Mathematics Teacher Education*, vol. 6 (2003).

Hirsch, E.D., *The Schools We Need: Why We Don't Have Them*. New York: Doubleday, 1996.

Johnson, Steven, *Emergence: The Connected Lives of Ants, Brains, Cities and Software*. New York: Scribner, 2001.

Kamii, Constance and Dominick, Ann, "The Harmful Effects of Algorithms in Grades 1–4." *National Council of Teachers of Mathematics Yearbook* (1998).

Kirschner, Paul A., Sweller, John and Clark, Richard E., "Why Minimal Guidance During Instruction Does Not Work: An Analysis of the Failure of Constructivist, Discovery, Problem-Based, Experiential and Inquiry-Based Teaching." *Educational Psychologist*, vol. 41, (2006).

Klein, David, "A Brief History of American K–12 Mathematics Education in the 20th Century." *Mathematical Cognition* (2003).

Kuhn, Thomas S., *The Structure of Scientific Revolutions*. Chicago: Chicago University Press, 1967.

Leinwand, Steve and Fleishman, Steve, "Research Matters / Teach Mathematics Right the First Time." *Teaching for Meaning*, vol. 62 (September 2004).

Ontario Ministry of Education, "Education for All: The Report of the Expert Panel on Literacy and Numeracy Instruction for Students With Special Education Needs, Kindergarten to Grade 6", 2005. Available at http://www.edu.gov.on.ca/eng/document/reports/ speced/panel/speced.pdf (accessed March 7, 2007).

Pesek, Dolores and Kirshner, David, "Interference of Instrumental Instruction in Subsequent Relational Learning." *Journal for Research in Mathematics Education*, vol. 31 (2000).

Phillips, D.C., "The Good, the Bad, and the Ugly: The Many Faces of Constructivism." *Educational Researcher*, vol. 24, no. 7 (1995).

Rosenshine, Barak, and Meister, Carla, "The Use of Scaffolds for Teaching Higher-Level Cognitive Strategies." *Educational Leadership* (April 1992).

Ross, Philip E., "The Expert Mind." *Scientific American* (July 2006).

Ruthven, Kenneth, "Ability Stereotyping in Mathematics." *Educational Studies in Mathematics*, vol. 18 (1987).

Schwartz, Jeffrey, and Begley, Sharon, *The Mind and the Brain: Neuroplasticity and the Power of Mental Force*. New York: Regan Books, 2002.

Shermer, Michael, "The Political Brain." *Scientific American* (July 2006).

Stiggins, Richard, "Assessment, Student Confidence and School Success." *Phi Delta Kappa*, http://www.pdkintl.org/kappan/k9911sti.htm (accessed March 7, 2007).

Suggate, Jennifer, "How Do They Do It? Children's Informal Methods of Addition and Subtraction." *Mathematics in School*, vol. 24 (1995).

Talbot, Margaret, "The Baby Lab: How Elizabeth Spelke Peers into the Infant Mind." *The New Yorker* (September 4, 2006).

Tobias, Sheila, *Overcoming Math Anxiety*. New York: W.W. Norton and Company, 1978.

Turner, J.C., Meyer, D.K., Midgely, C. and Patrick, H., "Teachers' Discourse and Sixth Grader's Reported Affect and Achievement Behaviours." *The Elementary School Journal*, vol. 103, 2003.

U.S. Department of Education. "'How Are the Children?' Report on Early Childhood Development and Learning," (1999). Available at http://www.ed.gov./pubs/How_Children/index.html (accessed March 7, 2007).

Waters, Ethan, "DNA Is Not Destiny: The New Science of Epigenetics Rewrites the Rules of Disease, Heredity and Identity." *Discover* (November 2006).

Wermuth, Paul Charles, *Modern Essays in Writing and Style*. New York: Holt, Rinehart and Winston, 1964.

Westley, Frances, Zimmerman, Brenda and Patton, Michael Q., *Getting to Maybe: How the World is Changed*. Toronto: Random House Canada, 2006.

Wheatley, Margaret, *Finding Our Way: Leadership For an Uncertain Time*. San Francisco: Barrett-Koehler Publishers, Inc., 2005.

White, Michael, and Gribbin, John, *Einstein: A Life in Science*. New York: Dutton, 1994.

Wilf, Herbert, "Can There Be 'Research in Mathematical Education'?" *Department of Mathematics. University of Pennsylvania*, http://www.wiskundemeisjes.nl/wp-content/uploads/2006/08/psutalk.pdf (accessed March 7, 2007).

Wiliam, Dylan, "Assessment for Learning: Why, What, and How?" *Orbit*, vol. 36, no. 2, (2006).

Wittgenstein, Ludwig, *Philosophical Investigations*. Oxford: Basil Blackwell, 1976.

Wu, H., "Basic Skills Versus Conceptual Understanding: A Bogus Dichotomy in Mathematics Education." *American Educator* (Fall 1999).

PERMISSIONS

Quotation on page 3 is from *Einstein: A Life in Science*.

Quotations on pages 27, 28, 88, 89 and 114 are from *The Mind and the Brain: Neuroplasticity and the Power of Mental Force*, published by HarperCollins. © 2002 Jeffrey Schwartz and Sharon Begley. Reprinted by permission.

Quotations on pages 44 and 45 are from "The Expert Mind" by Philip E. Ross, published in *Scientific American*, July 2006. Reprinted by permission.

Quotation on page 123 is from "Coxeter Theory: The Cognitive Aspects." Reprinted by permission.

Quotation on page 126 is from *The Character of Physical Law* by Richard Feynman, published by MIT Press.

Quotations on pages 163 and 171 are from *American Educator*.

Quotation on page 165 is from *Mathematical Cognition*.

Quotations on pages 218 and 219–20 are from *Journal for Research in Math Education*.

Quotations on pages 229, 230 and 233–34 are from "Politics and the English Language."

Quotation on page 258 is from *"Surely You're Joking, Mr. Feynman!"* by Richard Feynman, published by W.W. Norton & Company, Inc. Reprinted by permission.

Every effort has been made to contact the copyright holders; in the event of an inadvertent omission or error, please notify the publisher.

JOHN MIGHTON is a mathematician and the founder of JUMP Math—a system he developed for teaching and learning math. He is also an award-winning author and playwright. His first book, *The Myth of Ability: Nurturing Mathematical Talent in Every Child*, was a national bestseller. He lives in Toronto.